A HISTORY OF
SPARSHOLT AND LAINSTON

A History of
SPARSHOLT and
LAINSTON

by

CECILIA KNOWLES

PHILLIMORE

1981

Published by
PHILLIMORE & CO. LTD.
London and Chichester

Head Office: Shopwyke Hall,
Chichester, Sussex, England

ISBN 0 85033 396 2

Printed and bound in Great Britain by
GARDEN CITY PRESS LTD.
Letchworth, Herts.

CONTENTS

LIST OF ILLUSTRATIONS
(*between pages 112 and 113*)

ACKNOWLEDGEMENTS

The author would like to thank Miss Frances Collins for her help and encouragement over a long period; the Editor of the *Hampshire Chronicle* for permission to use the photographs of the village; the County Archivist and her Staff for help in research and the Librarian of Winchester Cathedral for permission to do research in the Cathedral Library. Above all, the Author is deeply indebted to Mr. David Johnston, of Southampton University, who was in charge of the Roman Villa Excavation, 1965-1972, and who wrote the account of this, Chapter 17, and the interpretation of the discoveries.

SPARSHOLT

ORIGIN OF THE NAME OF SPARSHOLT

Evidences of the people who lived here before villages were built can still be found and are marked on Ordnance maps, significantly adjacent to the branch of the Harroway that forms part of the western boundary of the parish. There are traces of round barrows on some of Moorcourt fields. Those marked on the Ordnance map just below West Wood are now obliterated by ploughing, but similar circles in the turf can be seen in dry weather below Privett Wood which is also on Moorcourt, just west of New Barn.

These people were Belgae who migrated from North France. Later immigrants than the Stone Age Goidels they brought with them the use of iron, arriving probably before 85 B.C.

*   *   *   *   *

There are at least two schools of thought regarding the origin of the name of Sparsholt. Dr. Ekwall in his *Dictionary of English Place Names* gives it a Saxon origin. He says that 'spar' came from spear, the shafts of which were made of wood, or from the spars for thatching which would be cut from the local woods. The suffix 'holt' means a woodland settlement.

Other authorities favour 'the chalk-stone wood', from Anglo-Saxon 'spar' and 'spar-stan'—chalk stone.

Dr. Andrews, the 19th-century Hampshire archaeologist, gave the name 'Speresholte' a Gaelic origin, meaning 'the sparse wood'.

VARIATIONS OF SPELLING

10th century.—Speoresholte.

11th century.—Spaersholte, Speresholte.

12th century.—Speresholte.

13th century.—As above; also Spereshoud, Spereshot, Spershot, Spersholt, Spersold, Sperisholt.

14th century.—As above; also Spereshot, Spirshotte, Spiesholte, Spersholte, Sparshot, Speresholte, Sperscholte.

15th century.—No specific variations.

16th century.—Spersholt, Sparshall, Spursholt.

17th century.—Sparshall, Sparshalt.

18th century.—Spirshott, Spersholt, Spershott, Sparshall, Sparshalt.

19th century.—Sparsoak, Sparoaks.

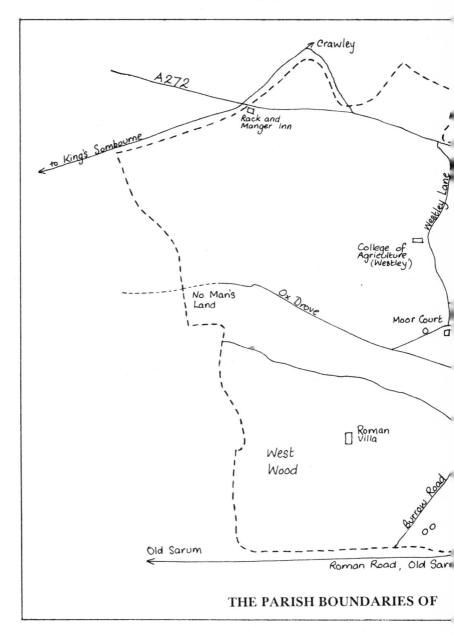

Crawley

A272

Rack and
Manger Inn

to King's Sombourne

Westley Lane

College of
Agriculture
(Westley)

No Man's
Land

Ox Drove

Moor Court

Roman
Villa

West
Wood

Burrow Road

Old Sarum

Roman Road, Old Sar

THE PARISH BOUNDARIES OF

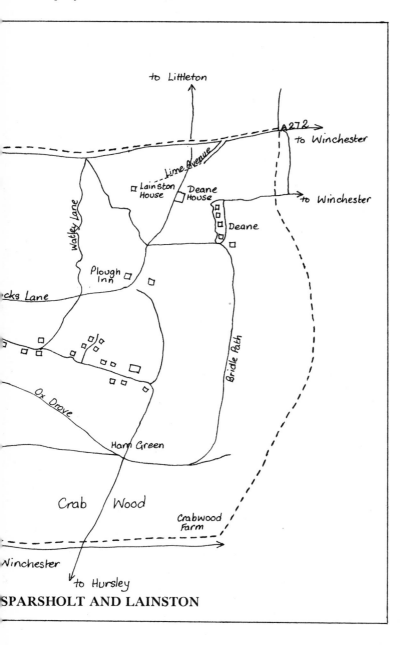

SPARSHOLT AND LAINSTON

Chapter One

TOPOGRAPHY

THE PARISH OF SPARSHOLT lies fairly high on the old downland which adjoined the ancient Forest of West Bere, one boundary point of which is indicated by the name of Deane, a hamlet in the parish. Lainston parish, 120 acres, lies to the north adjacent to Deane.

The highest point of both parishes, 450ft. above sea level, is the southern tip, where it runs close to Farley Mount. To the north the land slopes down through woods, remains of the Forest of West Bere, now made over to the Forestry Commission, to the fields of Moorcourt Farm. Northward again the land rises to the village which is mainly built on the 400ft. level. From here, except for sundry undulations, notably steeply down to Deane and up again towards Wyke Mark, the two parishes lie at an average of 350ft.

The soil has an all-over basis of chalk with a clay cap of varying depths starting roughly just west of Westley Farm (the Hampshire College of Agriculture), outlining the farm buildings in a deep 'V', missing out the lower fields, and running across to Moorcourt Farmhouse and its high ground. The clay also extends from the Westley fields north of Balldown Lane opposite Garstons, includes houses on Locks Lane and Home Lane, and narrows as it runs across the top of the hill to the village, stopping abruptly short of the church and the village street. East of this street the chalk rises to the surface and the old communal fields behind the *Woodman* inn (now a private house) must have been largely chalkland.

There are one or two small isolated clay caps marked by oak trees on Watley Farm and the pits at the top of Bushmoor Copse may be those from which, as legend has it, the clay for the bricks of Lainston House was dug.

Chapter Two

THE BOUNDARIES OF THE PARISHES

THE NEAREST POINT to Winchester of the parishes, taking the two as a whole, is at the Harestock/Salter Lane cross-roads to which the municipal boundary of the city now extends. Here Sparsholt has suffered the only alteration in its history. In 1932 the City of Winchester by Act of Parliament extended itself for about 120 yards west of the original boundary which ran along Salter Lane. The parish line now therefore runs from the A272 along the arable field instead of along the Lane, to the west of the little property called Terwick and across Deane Lane where it is marked with a concrete boundary stone, and continues the same distance west of Lanham Lane for about five-sixths of a mile.

About a quarter of a mile up this lane, just beyond where the Teg Down building estate joins it, the surface becomes unsuitable for a car. In places the boundary bank can be clearly seen on the west side of the lane and where the track from the old isolation hospital comes in the line crosses to the east side. An ancient lane with overgrown hedges, it winds upwards to Crab Wood Farm, runs close to the east wall of the farmhouse and across the garden to join a bank once marked by a line of old elms which runs for about 200 yards down the drive on the east side.

Where a short grass track leading to a field branches off on this side of the drive, the parish boundary crosses this track and follows the eastern side of the field till it reaches the edge of the Roman road from Winchester to Old Sarum. This part is now a modern road leading to Farley Mount, Ashley and the Sombournes. (The Romans coming with their new road from Winchester to Sarum followed the line in reverse of the far older South Hampshire Ridgeway which

2

came up from the coast via Mottisfont and the Test Valley, Parnholt Wood and Farley Mount to Winchester coming into the town over Teg Down.)

At the junction of field and road a boundary stone is marked on the Ordnance map, but has disappeared.

The parish boundary turns west with the road and follows the north bank along the edge of Crab Wood, probably the most ancient piece of woodland in the parish, as it was undoubtedly part of the medieval Forest of West Bere. The agger of the Roman road is here very noticeable.

Less than a quarter of a mile beyond the crossroads of the Sparsholt–Hursley road a boundary stone stands on the wood side. About the same distance further on the old Burrow Road comes up from Ham Green to join the Roman road. The name 'Burrow' is probably a corruption of 'Barrow' as not more than 150 yards from the junction of the two roads a round barrow can be clearly seen in the undergrowth, with possibly the remains of some smaller ones nearby.

About 150 yards further west the present road to Ashley and the Sombournes leaves the Roman road and follows roughly the line of the South Hampshire Ridgeway which runs past Farley Mount through Parnholt down to the Test Valley near Mottisfont.

Sparsholt parish boundary follows the Roman road which dips into a hollow of Pitt Down and runs west, only to be traced in places by the agger of the road, now a high bank, edging Forestry Commission plantations. At this point the Roman road ran within half a mile of the Villa (see Chapter 17) on the ridge to the north.

At the lowest part of the dip in the down, the agger has been cut through by Forestry working and the road's foundation of small flints superimposed on larger ones can be clearly seen. Here also, on the left, outlined by a double row of yews and a wide, shallow ditch, another pre-Roman road comes down from Standen Farm, which is in Hursley parish, crosses the South Hampshire Ridgeway to continue downhill across the Roman road as a grass track till in about half a mile it joins the branch of the Harroway that runs as part of the parish boundary from north to south.

The Roman road continues after the crossing of the road from Standen Farm in a straight line uphill, the parish boundary following it for about a quarter of a mile to the top of the ridge, then the boundary changes course abruptly and turns due south following roughly the line of the present wood of ancient beeches. The right-angle turn should also be marked by a boundary stone, which has disappeared. A slight bank marks the line through the trees to the top of the ridge, the South Hampshire Ridgeway and the road to Ashley, where at a boundary stone it swings suddenly almost due north to embrace in this acute angle a destroyed round barrow, known in local legend as Robin Hood's Butt.

The parish boundary follows a well-indicated bank along the edge of the beech trees and comes back to within a few yards of the Roman road and swings west with it.

At the western edge of the plantation the boundary turns due north and immediately crosses the Roman road as it debouches from the plantation on to the agricultural fields of Forest of West Bere Farm at which point it leaves the parish. The slight rise of the agger as it crosses the further field is clearly visible, and in a dry season the crop mark is clear.

The parish boundary is here at its most south-west and marches with that of Ashley. It runs due north for a little over a mile down between the Forestry Commission plantations and the fields. At certain points there are old boundary stones, some of them marked E.C. (Ecclesiastical Commissioners), and in the ridges of the plantation of Little West Wood there are scattered several granite marker stones with diagonal chiselling which may be others, or possibly boundary markers between Moorcourt, in Sparsholt, belonging to the Church Commissioners, and Hursley Park property. They have been so moved about by vandals that they no longer have any significance.

The 6-in. Ordnance map marks woods through which the parish boundary runs, but those on the west side of it have long been cleared and are now agricultural land, so the line actually runs between fields and woods for about one and a quarter miles to Corner Plantation and Sparsholt Corner, where there is a boundary stone.

Here it turns at right-angles west for about a quarter of a mile, then at right-angles north. At this point it meets the faint ghost of an old road marked as The Drove on the map, still with hedgerows, which less than fifty years ago was negotiable on foot. It ran west from this point to join another old track which linked it with the drove road running east from the Sombournes.

Turning north again at the junction with The Drove the parish line continues for about a quarter of a mile till it joins the above-mentioned drove road from the Sombournes. Round this junction lies No Mans Land, the original common grazing of the Sparsholt villagers. It is about a mile from the early communal fields of the parish.

At No Mans Land the parish boundary crosses the Sombourne track, which eastwards from this point is still marked on the map as The Drove, and continuing north follows the line of the ancient branch of the Harroway that ran from Finkley to the Test Valley at Fullerton, over Windmill Hill and to Winchester via Sparsholt. This, a 'summer way', joins the Sombourne track at No Mans Land and continues across Ham Green to Winchester. It is joined about 100 yards east of No Mans Land by the track that comes down from the South Hampshire Ridgeway across the Roman road.

Having skirted the western edge of No Mans Land, the parish boundary, following the line of the Harroway branch, goes north along the present iron fence between Moor Court Farm and the Up Sombourne fields along the edge of farmland to the crest of the down at about 350ft. above sea level. Here the Harroway branch becomes very clear; as a bridleway it leaves the fields into a grass lane bordered by high hedges in which nine different species have been identified giving the age of the hedges as about 900 years.

The lane drops to the 200ft. level and comes out on to the modern road from Kings Sombourne to the A272. Here on the left is a curious triangular piece of ground a few yards in extent, outlined on the track and road sides by straggling beech trees and a few old Scots pine, and on the arable field side by a wire fence. This plot of ground contains a suicide's grave.

Some time in the early 19th century an old woman called Mother Russell, living in the adjoining parish of Little Sombourne, suddenly committed suicide. It was said that she had long brooded over some crime that she had committed which had never been traced to her, but no one ever discovered the truth. As no suicide could be buried in consecrated ground she was buried at the junction of Little Sombourne and Sparsholt parishes.

At this point the parish boundary turns east along the Sombourne road and, crossing the A272 at *The Rack and Manger* inn, continues along a side road towards Crawley. In half a mile it turns south-east for about half a mile along another side road. A few yards short of its junction with the A272 the boundary takes a peculiar line turning east-south-east inside the roadside hedge and following what is now an unmarked line across a field, but which was originally the edge of a narrow belt of trees edging the field on the road side. It joins the further hedge about thirty yards above the road and continues north-east along this hedge. Halfway along the second hedge in from the road the boundary meets a hedgerow at right-angles on Northwood Park. Here it turns south-south-east and follows the hedgerow and the bank, which in places is clearly visible, till it joins the Northwood Road (or Balldown Drive) just below Winsleigh House.

It crosses this private road, goes through the field gate and turns at right-angles south-south-west, running on another unmarked line a few yards in from the hedge to cross the gardens of Balldown Cottages and join a bank beyond straight down to the A272 along which it swings almost due east.

Up to now the boundary line has been of Sparsholt parish only, but in less than a quarter of a mile it meets that of Lainston at the junction of Watley Lane. This lane was originally part of the boundary between the two parishes, Lainston parish being only 120 acres in extent, but the two are now combined.

Following the line of Lainston along the A272 from Watley Lane the boundary climbs a steep little hill on the crest of which is the main entrance of Lainston House on the right and on the left that to the now-demolished Northwood Park.

Dropping down the hill to Sparsholt Cross the boundary leaves Lainston at this point and rejoins Sparsholt, continuing along the A272 up another short hill where on the right can be seen the end of the famous three-quarter-mile long lime avenue that runs north-east from Lainston House, mentioned by John Evelyn, grandson of the diarist, in July 1714.

The parish boundary follows the A272 towards Winchester and at the Harestock/Salter Lane crossroads meets the starting point of the boundary walk.

Chapter Three

ANCIENT RIGHTS OF WAY

SPARSHOLT has a number of old footpaths and bridleways. One of them, Burrow, or Barrow, Road runs as a bridleway from Ham Green almost due south to join the Farley Mount Road near where the modern highway swings left from the line of the Roman road. The first few yards of Burrow Road as it leaves Ham Green have been diverted to accommodate an entrance to new bungalows. Close to the start of Burrow Road on the opposite side of the Sparsholt-Hursley road a footpath crosses Ham Green and starts diagonally uphill to Crabwood Farm.

From Deane at the right-angle turn at the foot of the hill down from Sparsholt a bridleway leads up towards Crabwood Farm and crossing the east end of Ham Green continues straight up the hill to the farm. At the crossing a rider can turn left and north and join the lane from Deane to Wyke at the top of Deane Hill.

Halfway down the hill from Sparsholt to Deane a stile in the right-hand bank leads on to a path that crosses the farm fields below Sparsholt Manor garden and comes out at the School below the Memorial Hall. From here it crosses the village street and opposite the Post Office follows a narrow path leading to Home Lane. Crossing this by Pies Cottage it continues to Locks Lane which it crosses and enters the Cricket Field. Running along the eastern edge of this it crosses a stile and turning at the corner of Grove Copse and Bushmoor Copse continues straight down to the Stockbridge Road, A272.

From No Man's Land on the western boundary of the parish, the partially-metalled farm road running east continues the line of the track from the Sombournes which has been joined by the Harroway branch and from the south by the one from Standen. These continue east as Ox Drove, crossing the Sparsholt-Hursley lane at Ham Green which is common

8

land, and eastwards as a green lane about 30 yards wide. A little under a mile eastwards it is crossed by a lane dropping down from Crabwood Farm which continues downhill to emerge at Deane, a hamlet of Sparsholt. This land and the Ham Green track are reputedly the ways along which the 19th-century smugglers brought their goods up from the coast by the South Hampshire Ridgeway, hiding them in emergency in the cellars of certain houses in Deane.

From the cross-lanes above, Ham Green (Ox Drove) runs downhill and then rises steeply to the top of Deane Hill where it joins the steep, narrow lane from Deane itself and continues eastwards to Wyke Mark, Weeke and Winchester.

The King Billy Alehouse

Before the Ox Drove reaches Ham Green and slightly short of the lane up to Moorcourt, a now almost obliterated track, known as Bull Drove, rises on the left as a double hedgerow 120ft. to 400ft. level and is the boundary of Westley (Hampshire College of Agriculture) and Moor Court Farms, to join the present Westley Lane from Sparsholt village to A272 at Balldown. At the summit of its climb the old land from Ox Drove came out on to flat land and here were an alehouse known as *The King Billy*, two old cottages and a windmill.

Leaving the site of the *King Billy* the double hedgerow runs north to end in Westley Lane, about 50 yards east of the entrance drive to the Hampshire College of Agriculture, Westley Farm. At this entrance another footpath starts and continues down the drive to turn west through the farm buildings of Westley Farm and out along a farm track for about ¼ mile till it begins to rise to the ridge beyond along the left side of a quick-set hedge. At the top of the ridge there is a stile in the hedge after crossing which the footpath follows the headland across two fields to a boundary gate. The path here leaves Westley and until this was obliterated by ploughing in 1977 followed a grass lane between hedges down to A272 where there is a stile and a footpath marker.

Lastly a footpath starts from the road opposite Lainston Home Farm and runs up to the hill top where it ends in the Winchester-Stockbridge road (A272).

Chapter Four

THE MANOR AND THE MANOR COURTS

SPARSHOLT was never a separate manor. When in 633 King Cynegils of Wessex, the first Christian king, knew he was dying, he left to the Church of Winchester all the land round the city within seven leagues distance. After his death Cynewalh, his son, in 639 simplified the bequest by granting to the Benedictine Abbot of Winchester the whole of the great manor of Chilcomb. This included Chilcomb itself, Morestead, St. Faith (Winchester), Compton, Weeke, Winnal, Littleton, and Sparsholt. Later they were merged in the great Manor of Barton and Buddlesgate with a total area of 608 hides. Besides the eight churches mentioned there appear to have been others, long since vanished, which were included in the manor.

The entry in Domesday is:

Ciltecombe

The Bishop of Winchester holds Ciltecombe. In the time of King Edward it was as now assessed at 1 hide. Here are 68 ploughlands. 12 in demesne and 30 villeins and 115 borderers with 57 ploughlands; also nine churches, 20 servants, 4 mills worth £4, 40 acres of meadow herbage which pays 23/5d and woods for the pannage of 30 hogs.

Of this manor William holds land enough for 2 ploughs, and Manno held it: Cheping enough for 1 plough and he held it before, Walter holds land enough for 1 plough which was held by Ælfer: Hugh the Sexton holds enough for 2 ploughs held by Giraud. Turstin Rufus holds enough for 1 plough which was held by Ædmer; Osborn holds enough for 1 plough which was held by Godwin; and Turstin the Younger holds 30 acres which were held by Ælfec. Those who held these lands in the time of King Edward could not remove to another lord. The present tenants have 7 ploughlands in demesne and there are 7 villeins and 30 borderers with 2 ploughlands; also 11 servants and 4 acres of

10

meadow. The whole manor was worth, in the time of King
Edward and afterwards, £73. What the monks hold is of the
value of £80, and what is held by others £24. There were 6 hides
adjoining this manor in the time of King Edward, which Ralph
de Mortimer now holds; but he owes no service to the church.

The above refers to the entire manor and details of
Sparsholt and the other parishes are not given, but the first
entry in Sparsholt baptism register which begins in 1607 is
of an infant Godwin who just conceivably might have been a
descendant of him who had held 'land enough for one
plough' before Osborn succeeded, or perhaps ousted, him.

Stigand, Bishop of Winchester, 1047-1052, granted a
hide of land in Sparsholt to Aethelmere, a thegn, and to his
son, Saeman. The land actually belonged to the Old Minster,
the original monastic foundation of Winchester, and one
copy of the charter was deposited in the Old Minster.

Small as it was, Sparsholt was divided into certainly two
minor manors, Westley being one and Deane another. There
is also a mention of Fromond's Court, later merged with
Lainston, which was not included in the Manor of Chilcomb.

The whole manor which included Sparsholt, was known
as Moorcourt (Morecourt, Merecourt) and was the property
of the Prior and monks of St. Swithun's Monastery in
Winchester. Their successors after the Dissolution of the
Monasteries were the Dean and Chapter of Winchester
Cathedral, who held it till 1862, when it became the property
of the Ecclesiastical Commissioners, later the Church Commissioners.

Justice was administered in Saxon times by various courts.
The Hundred of Buddlesgate in which Sparsholt lies, would
have been administered by the Court of the Hundred
(Hundred-Mote), a court for anyone who had a complaint,
and was held by its own Hundred Men under the writ of the
Sheriff. Later, when the more important cases were decided
by the Shire Mote, the Hundred Mote was reduced in importance and tried only petty offences. In late Saxon times
there came in smaller sub-divisions, the teothings, or tythings.
In these every man whose rank and property were not sufficient to guarantee his good behaviour was compelled after

the reign of Athelstan (925–939) to find someone who would guarantee him. The members of a certain tything formed a sort of perpetual bail for each other's appearance in case of crime, with apparent final responsibility if the criminal escaped or if his estate was insufficient to pay his fine.

The tything man for the parish was elected each year at the September Manor Court and served for one year.

The Manor of Barton, etc.

On 1 May 1541, Henry VIII granted to the Dean and Chapter of Winchester 'such estates and other sources of revenue as might support their due estate'. By 1541 Chilcombe had been included with all its subsidiary manors amounting to some 13,639 acres in the Manor of Barton Priors. The king granted to the Dean and Chapter most of the manors formerly belonging to St. Swithun's Monastery with all manorial and other rights. This manor included 'The great manor of Berton, including Chiltcombe, Hanglecombe, Avington, Morstead, Wylehall (Winnall), Nova Villa (the Soke of Winchester), Spersholte, Wyke, Cumptone, Drayton, and Sparkeford St. James, Fulflood, Bradelygh, outside Kingsgate, Kyngate Strete and Gyngestre Strete and Brexedona (Buxden)'.

A second Letter of Patent of 1 May 1541 granted all manors, messuages, lands and tenements and rents in the same villages to the Dean and Chapter, including the ancient pension now called a rent charge of 2s. from Sparsholt rectory.

Yet a third Letter Patent of the same date granted the Manor of Moorecourt with all rights, members and appurtenances as well as every other kind of manorial right to the Dean and Chapter, but the Crown reserved to itself the fee of 3s. 4d. to the Collector of Rents and Farms at Moorecourt. The manor was valued annually at £7 12s. 6d.

The Manor of Westley

Lying at the extreme west end of the parish Westley was possibly not included in the Manor of Chilcomb at the time of King Cynegil's gift in 633 to the Prior and monks of

St. Swithun's at Winchester, though it may have been included in the land sold into private hands between 1050 and 1060 by Stigand, Bishop of Winchester. The Manor of Westley was granted to the Coldrey family in the 13th or 14th centuries and later passed to the Skillings of Lainston.

Westley Farm, as it now is, consists of about 437 acres and is the Hampshire College of Agriculture.

Of the ancient farm buildings very little remains except for a delightful small manor house, much altered, and probably much older than the earliest known date—1845— and some flint and brick farm buildings dated 1871.

Chapter Five

THE COMPOTUS ROLLS, 1308-1842

THE COMPOTUS ROLLS of the Manor of Barton and Buddlesgate, in which Sparsholt was included, run from 1308 to 1842, though for the last hundred years the only items mentioned are the names of the tithing men elected for the year.

By the time the earliest Rolls begin Sparsholt and the Manor of Chilcomb (608 hides) in which it was included had been absorbed into the Manor of Barton and Buddlesgate which was also the name of the Hundred. When surveyed in the 1890s the acreage of Sparsholt was 3,542 acres.

As by far the largest house in the village of Sparsholt was Morecourt (Moorcourt and Merecourt), on the western edge of the village, it is almost certain that the Manor Courts were held there. In 1682 the account of the Court business was described as of Morecourt Manor, but it is still included in the Hundred Rolls in the Manor of Barton and Buddlesgate.

The Manor belonged to the Prior and Monks of St. Swithun at Winchester as it had since the gift of King Cynegils in 633 together with the rest of the Manor of Chilcomb. King Edgar the Elder had confirmed the gift in 908. It has descended direct from them, through the Dean and Chapter of Winchester Cathedral, to the modern Church Commissioners.

As the parish was small and unimportant nothing much is to be gained in knowledge of the village life from the Rolls though it is interesting to see the early dates at which some of the well-known Sparsholt surnames are first mentioned and from the context are not new arrivals. Of these are John Godewyn (Godwin), 1482; Nicholas Locke, 1482; Thomas Browning, 1475; John Blake, 1536; Richard Kene,

14

or Kean, 1389; John Fromond, 1418; Robert Buxey, 1596; and John Fielder, 1699.

There is a gap in the Rolls from 1324 to 1338 and from 1344–1362. The latter is probably due to the Black Death (1348) during the course of which over several years Winchester diocese had the third largest death roll in the country, only Ely and Norwich dioceses being more severely hit. It was reckoned that 48 per cent. of the beneficed clergy died.

In 1308, the earliest date for recorded court proceedings, the Assize Rents (rents of fixed amounts) for Sparsholt totalled £12 6s. 1¼d. By 1339 this had only increased to £12 6s. 8¼d., and was still the same in 1392.

Assize Rents

						£	s.	d.
1308	..	..	..	..	..	12	6	1¼
1318	..	..	..	.:	..	12	6	7¼
1324	..	..	..	..	..	12	6	7¼
1338	..	..	..	..	..	12	6	8¼
1339	..	..	..	..	..	12	6	8¼
1476	..	..	..	..	..		9	2
1548	..	..	..	..	..	21	11	6
1552	..	..	..	..	..	21	11	6
1554	..	..	..	..	..	21	11	6

The long gap between 1476 and 1548, with a sudden rise in Assize Rents, when the Rolls begin again, from 9s. 2d. to £21 11s. 6d., points to a considerable rise in land values or perhaps a more efficient Steward. After 1554 no further totals of Assize Rents are given.

It appears that the monastic officials were not very efficient in recording facts and transactions in what was a small entity in a large manor. Whether there was a bailiff, or bedell, especially for Sparsholt is uncertain. Only once (1392) is the bedell named, Nicholas Menchone. He was the equivalent of a village policeman and was also responsible for taking pledges from the villagers as well as letting certain individuals know when and where they were due to appear on the lord's land for seasonal works.

There is mention of, but not by name, a reeve in 1339, and occasionally thereafter. He was effectually the lord's representative in the village and was in charge of the work on his land. In the same casual fashion there is mention from time to time of a bailiff and rent collector. (Collector of Rents—William Yelderwyle, 1509; Thomas Shaft, 1525; Richard Browning, 1553.)

Life in the village proceeded on its quiet way enlivened by an occasional brawl or prohibited cutting of timber in the lord's woods. Thomas More was fined 4d. in 1533 for cutting down one oak on his own land without the lord's licence. Two others were fined 6d. each for cutting underwood in 'Empnolt' without permission. An escape from the manor by a villein (1505) no doubt roused feelings of admiring envy in the hearts of his contemporaries; if he could remain outside uncaught for a year and a day he could not be forced to return to the manor. If he was caught the fine was one penny. Another hard burden borne by the villeins was that they could not give their daughters in marriage to anyone outside the village without the lord's licence, for which, of course, they had to pay.

In spite of what must have been a perpetual dearth of actual cash the peasants did sometimes manage to pay for release from plough service and other works on the lord's land. In 1392 Robert Waryn paid 7s. 7½d. for 1 messuage and virgate of land instead of plough service, and in that year also 11 others paid sums varying from 15s. 7½d. to 3s. 9½d. for this privilege.

When all animals had a definite cash value in addition to their owners dependence on them for meat, milk and draught work, it is surprising how frequently they were found straying and remaining unclaimed sometimes for months, until they were finally sold off by the reeve.

In 1362 a 'draught animal strayed since last midsummer' was still unclaimed at the September court. At Midsummer 1418 'a white hog priced 12d. straying from the time of the last court to remain with the lord because unclaimed then sold to John Dene for same price'. In those days of crushing poverty and near starvation in winter it would seen that even the fencing in of their animals was beyond the villeins, and if their beasts could stay their hunger on a neighbour's strip all the better as long as the owner was not found out. The animals themselves were probably near-skeletons by the end of a severe winter.

Enclosures

There does not seem to have been any hardship due to enclosure awards, in fact, there were none enforced, though by exchange agreement several small owners consolidated their holdings. An example is in the Court Rolls of December 1755 when

William Hewett	..	..	..	..	58a. 1r. 2p.
Richard Blake	..	..	..	..	2 pieces of 56a. 13p.
Mary Browning	..	..	..	..	3 pieces 51a. 1r. 28p.
					1 piece 1a. 2r. 13p.
Thomas Blake	..	..	..	..	1 piece 3a. 2p.

All copyholders of Barton Manor and

Anne Bassett leaseholder 3 pieces 48a. 8r., holders of land in small allotments in Dean Field, Sparsholt, have agreed to enclose Dean Field for improvement.

Chapter Six

THE CHURCH OF ST. STEPHEN

THE CHURCH stands on a knoll at the extreme end of a low ridge of clay that finishes in the centre of the village. This position points to a very early date for the first church, probably built like the houses around it of wattle and daub, and on a pagan holy site. It was the custom of the early Christian missionaries to take over the place which the heathen population already venerated.

Confirmation of this was found in 1883 ·when major repairs were carried out. The south-west corner of the church was found to have no foundations, but to be resting on an open grave. The Rev. Evelyn Heathcote, the vicar, noted this in his manuscript history of the parish, but said that he could not speak as to the condition of the skeleton. Possibly the workmen lifted it before he arrived on the scene. The fact of the angle of the wall resting on a grave indicates the ancient custom of sacrifice to ensure stability for the building.

Baring Gould in *Strange Survivals* (1892) describes this custom dating from remote pagan times. A sacrifice of some sort was offered at the laying of the foundation of a building and also at its completion—even a church was 'laid in blood' —or the walls would not stand. The sacrifice was offered to the god under whose protection the building was placed. Some animal was placed under the corner stone—dog, cow, wolf, black cock, or goat—sometimes the body of a malefactor who had been executed. The custom originated when man first built permanent homes instead of those of poles and skins which could be moved, for in making foundations he was disturbing the face of Mother Earth and thus securing to himself a portion of the earth's surface which had been given by her to all her children in common. Therefore he first offered her a propitiatory sacrifice. This custom prevailed into the Middle Ages. Human sacrifice was certainly sometimes made, as is proved in the authentic story of the skeleton found under the corner of a wall in the church of Holsworthy, Devon (Baring Gould, *op. cit.*).

A further example of an ancient rite was discovered also in 1883 when an 8ft. extension to the chancel was made. Workmen digging foundations came upon the bones of a horse. This was not an unusual early rite for a churchyard. A live horse was buried to symbolise the Pale Horse of the Apocalypse which waits to carry the souls of the dead to the nether regions. It was also the horse of the god Woden, god of the dead, who carried off souls on his Hell-Horse.

Apart from these discoveries there is the local tradition of a Saxon church on the site and that foundations survive in the north-west corner. If this is so they are now demolished or buried under Butterfield's north aisle, added in 1883-4.

In 1204 a court was convened to settle a dispute which had been going on for more than a year between John de Caritate and Alan de Spersholte about the advowson of the church (Curia Regis Roll 65, 1204). It is not known how the case was finally settled, but the jurors' evidence is interesting. The eleventh juror, William de Hattingele, said that Godfrey de Caritate, father of John, 'had built the aforesaid church of stone and chalk'. (The Latin is *petra et calce,* i.e., stone and limestone, but almost certainly means stone and chalk which was more locally available than genuine limestone, though *silex* is correct Latin for chalk.) Chalk was probably, therefore, the material of which the walls of Godfrey de Caritate's church were built, as it is the stone of which the Norman south-aisle pillars are made. The lower courses of the south-western buttress of the tower, built in 1480, were of the same material prior to 1883.

William de Hattingele was asked if he remembered a church of wood and replied that he had heard tell of it but had never seen it. Richard de Anisie, twelfth juryman, supported him, adding that Thomas Oislun had told him the same thing.

There is a theory that this dispute was about the advowson
of the church at Lainston, but as Lainston church is a mile
to the north and in a separate manor it could never have
been the church of Sparsholt parish. The argument put
forward is that Godfrey de Caritate would never have built
a church at Sparsholt as the advowson was in the possession
of the Cistercian Nunnery of Hartley Wyntney. It is not
known, however, when the advowson was presented to
that priory which was itself only founded in 1200. The first
certain date for a prioress is Lucy, 1225.

At whatever date the priory was presented with the
advowson of Sparsholt this must have been after the building
of Godfrey de Caritate's church. The jurymen in 1204
remembered the building of the church of stone and chalk
'a good many years previously' and in addition they remembered that Godfrey had presented to the living one Robert,
who had lived 'more than eighty years'. This would have
been a phenomenal incumbency even in an age when an
acolyte could receive his first Holy Orders at the age of
12, but goes to show that the de Caritates had had the
advowson and the right to build a church long before the
Priory of Hartley Wyntney was founded.

There was probably first a timber church in Saxon times.
The parish had been included with several others in the
Manor of Chilcomb given to the Prior and Monks of the St.
Swithun's Abbey in Winchester by the Saxon King Cynegils
in 633. The earliest remains of parts of 12th-century walls
are to be found in the north-west corner of the tower (built
in 1480) which is long and short work from top to bottom,
typically Saxon, and is possibly material re-used.

In about 1211 the south aisle was added, a simple Norman
arcade of three arches with plain capitals to the chalk pillars.
The second pillar from the east has on it several scratched
dates, one of them 1692 with the last two figures reversed
and there are some crosses carved on this and the next pillar.
In the outside of this south wall are several Roman bricks,
and it is probable that some of the flints of which the wall is
principally built came from the same source, the ruined
Roman Villa on the ridge of West Wood, about a mile away.

Also on the south wall, close to the now blocked priest's door, is a scratch dial which may be of the same date as the wall. It is crude, but still clear, and the hole for the gnomon will hold a thin peg. In its worn condition it is impossible to say that one line is more deeply incised than any other to show the hour of Mass.

In 1367 the chancel was rebuilt to equal the width of the nave and the now blocked priest's door into the sanctuary probably dates from this period.

The chancel arch as it is today is late 16th century but has a peculiar feature that the lower part of the arch up to 5ft. 7½ins. is of an entirely different character to the rest of the jamb. It is possible that the lower section is some of the original 12th-century work which was moved outwards when the chancel was widened in 1367.

John Fromond

John Fromond (d. 1420) was a native of Sparsholt and had been bailiff to William of Wykeham (Bishop of Winchester, 1367–1404) and his predecessor William Edyngton (1345–1366). Fromond's father and grandfather had also served the Bishops of Winchester. He owned land in the Sombournes, Stockbridge and Waltham, as well as Sparsholt where he had land and tenements and a considerable amount of stock.

He founded a chantry dedicated to St. Catherine in Sparsholt church and appointed a chaplain in perpetuity to say Masses for his soul and that of his wife. As at that time the only place for such a chantry would have been the south aisle there can be little doubt that John Fromond's chantry stood at the east end of this aisle. It was probably destroyed in about 1550 when under Edward VI all chantries were suppressed by the Act of 1547. In 1967 a chapel to St. Catherine was dedicated in the same position.

The east window in this aisle has some tracery that certainly dates from the time of Fromond and the chapel would have fitted in well between the entrance porch in its original position, halfway along the south wall and the east end of the aisle.

*   *   *   *   *

In about 1480 the tower was built at the west end of the church. The eastern arch has continuous mouldings similar to the chancel arch and its Perpendicular west window, though patched and renewed, has two 15th-century cinquefoil lights with a quatrefoil in the head. (See 'Windows' on page 28.)

The main entrance door is dated 1631. Though no longer in its original position halfway along the south wall it has above it the inscription:

Anno 1631
John Higeng) Churchwardens
William Hobes)

In 1721 Mr. William Merrill of Lainston and a Mr. Hobbs Weeks presented an oak gallery which was put up at the west end at the entrance to the tower. According to the Rev. Evelyn Heathcote, writing in 1883, 'It considerably darkened the church and provided about thirty uncomfortable sittings where boys and men used to go and frequently behave badly'.

It was removed in 1884 during the alterations to the church.

In 1764 the oak beam that spans the chancel arch was put up. The inscription on it is:

W.M.   1764.   I.F.

This probably gives the initials of the churchwardens. The vicar was the Rev. Richard Barford. This beam may once have supported a rood, or, if the chancel had become dilapidated as so often happened in its long history, the beam may have been needed to tie the fabric together.

In 1842, when the Rev. William Masters died at the age of 94 having been vicar for 48 years, the church was in appallingly bad repair. The chancel was evidently disproportionately small. When Sir William Heathcote of Hursley Park, holder of the great tithe, planned repairs in 1843 he referred to his responsibility for 'my little chancel'.

The total repairs, including new pews and flooring, cost £270, of which Sir William contributed £120. The rest was raised by a parish rate and private subscription.

There was a plan, fortunately not carried out, to restore a screen that had formerly stood in front of the 'Lainston Pew' at the east end of the south aisle and occupied most of this space. It was 'a sort of room with battlemented front and a separate ceiling', according to the Rev. Evelyn Heathcote. At one time the whole of the south aisle had been known as the Lainston Aisle. Nothing is known of the origin of this screen which might have been a relic of the Fromond Chantry, and it has disappeared.

On the death of the vicar, Mr. Stewart, in 1875, the church was again in disrepair. The new vicar, the Rev. Evelyn Heathcote, son of Sir William Heathcote, called in the well-known architect, Mr. William Butterfield. He estimated the cost of the repairs as £2,372, which by 1885 was completely paid off by the parish.

When the work began it was found that a mass of soil had accumulated round the west and north walls to a height of what is now the sill of the west window in the tower, approximately 7ft. This soil was removed and with its dispersal the grave mentioned earlier was found at the south-west corner of the church.

Mr. Heathcote noted that the position of the string course surrounding the tower and the fact that the great buttress at the south-west angle was found on excavation to be built on rough chalk blocks it seemed that the west and north sides of the church had always been built against the earth. (It is possible that these chalk blocks may be relics of Godfrey de Caritate's first stone church.) The building of 1480 was of poor workmanship. At probably the same date the erection of the great buttress of the tower had caused the crushing of the arch into the tower which had then been solidly filled in with brickwork leaving merely an entrance into a cavity, later made into a coal-hole, which was situated below the platform on which the bell-ringers stood. The level of this entrance was approximately at the level of the sill of the west window. All this was cleared away and the tower left as it is today, strengthened and with the addition of the wooden belfry and spire.

During the repairs inside the church portions of the older walls came to light. These were in many cases carved and coloured a rich red with other parts gilded. Some of this work was found in the east wall of 1480 and on this, north of the altar, a mutilated fresco of St. Stephen with a stone canopy above it. When first uncovered the fresco was seen to be brightly coloured in red, bluish green and primrose yellow. The colours unfortunately faded on exposure to the light, but Mrs. Heathcote made a watercolour which still exists, of both fresco and canopy. At some time, probably during the Civil War, some vandal had deliberately destroyed the face of the saint, his tool marks being plainly visible. In 1883 no process was known for preserving a fresco, so, as the east wall had to be pulled down to lengthen the chancel by 8ft., the painting had to be destroyed. The canopy is now above the south doorway.

The chancel appeared to have been shortened by nearly one half at some time, and the walls covered with plaster and hung with slates in their exposed parts to keep out the wet.

As well as the medieval colours in the walls Mr. Heathcote found beneath the plaster traces of frescoed lettering, particularly round the windows which were 'surrounded with bold flowing scrolls in rich red and bright yellow ochre and on part of the walls there were texts in black-letter of a later date'.

He also noted that 'the remains of the older church which were found were placed in the belfry'. It is possible that he was referring to the flat-topped arch that now stands above the arch into the tower which may have been part of a doorway, but nothing is known of its original place in the church. It seems to be Tudor. (It has recently [1978] been filled in with the royal arms sculpted and painted by Mr. Brian Walker, presented by Mrs. Robert Bostock in memory of her husband.)

The most important discovery at this time was the grave of a 12th- or 13th-century priest which was found during the erection of scaffolding inside the church. A pole broke suddenly into a grave which was below the floor close to the 'reading desk'. From the position on a plan this refers to the pulpit.

Immediately below the hole made by the scaffolding pole was the body of a priest in a chalk coffin, the burial wrappings still intact about the feet. Buried with him were a pewter chalice and paten which had a crude cross inscribed on it. Both are still in the possession of the church. These vessels are very similar to those found in the church of Berwick St. James, in Wiltshire, which are in the British Museum.

The chalk coffin was removed and placed against the south wall outside the blocked-up priest's door into the sanctuary.

The 18th-century gallery was taken down in 1883, part of it being made into a screen between the chancel and what was at that time the organ chamber with the vestry to the east completing the wall line of the north aisle which was built on at this time. This part of the gallery, a plain dark oak cornice and three simple tapering pillars topped by plain capitals, still remains between the chancel and the Lady Chapel, but the rest of the material was disposed of and two pillars are to be seen in the drawing room of Helston House in Sparsholt.

When all the alterations and additions were completed the measurements of the church were:

Chancel	..	..	24ft. 6in. x 19ft. 6in.
Nave..	..	..	36ft. x 19ft. 6in.
Tower	..	..	9ft. square.

The church was re-consecrated and an addition to the churchyard consecrated by the Bishop of Winchester on 10 July 1883.

Though the chamber for an organ was made in 1882–3 for another five years the singing was, as before, led by the parish clerk blowing the bassoon which, until it was stolen in December 1978, was preserved in a glass case at the west end of the church. An organ was not bought until 1887 when Walker and Son supplied one at a cost of £250. This, plus £25 for carriage and installing, were all paid off together with the rest of the expenses by December 1887.

Presumably by Mr. Butterfield, the parish was persuaded to remove from beneath the altar and the floor of the sanctuary the slabs marking the tombs of William Baker (vicar, 1685-1731) and his wife, Jane, and daughter, Jane; also that of Edward Lane, (vicar, 1655-1685), Henry Lane and Edward Lane, his sons; and William Masters (vicar, 1794-1842) and his wife, Ann. The gravestones were placed as a form of flooring in the base of the tower, there to be trampled on by bell-ringers and choir so that they are now much damaged. They have now been covered with coconut matting. The inscriptions are as follows:

Within the altar rails on the south side

> Under this stone in the dust resteth the bodies of
> Jane the Mother and Jane the daughter of
> William Baker, Vicar of this parish.
> Jane the Mother dyed July 12 1696 aged 81 (or 83)
> (or) in ye 81st (or 83rd) year ...
> [this is almost illegible]
> Jane the daughter dyed July 9 1726
> aged 36 (?) (or) in ye 36th year ...
> [this is almost illegible]

Next to it to the north

> Under this stone lies the body of
> William Baker
> Who was 46 years Vicar of this parish
> and dyed Nov. 12 1731 aged 82
> Also the ..dy of Jane Baker (?) widow
> and relict of the said W.... Baker
> Who dyed the 2nd of June 1734,

Next to it to the north (or beneath the altar as some accounts state)

> Under this stone
> expecting a happy
> Resurrection in Xt
> lieth in   Revd Edward Lane
> of the Flock for 50 years
> the faithful pastor
>   Come Lord Jesus
> Died 2nd of September 1685
> In the 81st year of his age.

(Mrs. Mary Lane, his wife, was buried before him in the same grave, 27 October 1669.)

Under the north wall of the chancel within the altar rails

> Here lieth ye body of Mr.
> Edward Lane who was
> ye son of Mr. Edward Lane
> Vicar of this Parish
> He died May . . .
> Mrs. Jane Lane hath laid this epitaph
> And stone upon her deare husband's grave
> Who having Ireland . . . seene . . .
> Hither Hee came to Travell unto Heaven

(This stone, even in 1876 was almost totally illegible except for the part words Pro and Sch. From the entry in the register it is almost certainly the stone over the grave of Henry Lane, son of the vicar, Edward Lane.)

The register states that 'Henry Lane sonne of ye Vicar of this parish and a probationer scholar of New College, Oxon was buried here in the chancel behind the reading pew Oct. 6th 1659, born 1639'.

A further entry in the register notes 'Mr. Edward Lane ye eldest sonne of ye Vicar of this Parish was buried by his brother May 17th 1660'.

A large black slab in the chancel outside the altar rails

> Here lie the remains of
> Ann wife of
> The Revd. William Masters M.A.
> Vicar of this Parish
> who departed this life
> August 24 1825
> 　　　Aged 61
> Here also lie the remains of
> The Revd. William Masters
> Vicar of this Parish
> who departed this life
> April 1. 1842.
> 　　　Aged 93.

While the Rev. Clifford Dalhousie Ramsay was vicar (1904-1918) plans were drawn up to erect a chancel screen in memory of two vicars, Evelyn Heathcote (1875-1893) and Francis Ainger (1893-1904). The architect was Mr. G. H. Kitchin, and the screen was made by Thomas and Co. of Winchester. It is of carved wood decorated in coloured gesso, this latter work being carried out by Mrs. and Miss Heathcote, widow and sister of the late vicar. The north half is dedicated to Mr. Ainger with on the cornice his coat-of-arms and that of his college, St. John's, Cambridge. On the cornice are shields bearing the emblems of the Passion.

Below the balustrading of the north half of the screen is a painted panel with a boat in full sail moving towards the sunset and below it the text, 'So He bringeth them to the Haven where they would be'. Beneath the text is inscribed:

In Memory of
Francis Edward Ainger
Vicar of this Parish
1893–1904

On the south side a corresponding panel is painted with a black bird singing to the rising sun with the date May Day 1908. Beneath on a scroll is inscribed 'Let me go for the day breaketh'.

In Memory of Evelyn Dawsonne Heathcote
Vicar of this Parish
1875–1893

The screen was subscribed for by relations of the two vicars, and by friends and parishioners who had known them. The Bishop of Winchester dedicated it at a service held on 1 May 1910.

The Windows

East Window in Chancel

This still has some of its original tracery, but the original glass has long since disappeared. The present window dates from the late 19th century and was put up in memory of Charles Barrington Barnes and Julia Harriett Everett. They were the brother and sister of Mr. Scott Barnes of Lainston. The window is composed of three lancets, the central one with Christ in Glory, the empty tomb below His feet. The north lancet has the Saints John and Peter, the south the Blessed Virgin and St. Mary Magdalen. Above each group hovers an angel holding a hanging scroll with on it 'Why seek the living among the dead?'. Beneath all three lancets 'Christ has risen from the dead and become the first fruits of them that slept'.

The tracery of the south windows in the chancel is 15th century, the easternmost having three cinquefoil lights and the south-western two lights in typical 15th-century tracery but with a new mullion.

The east window in the south aisle has some tracery dating from the time of John Fromond (15th century). His chantry would have fitted in conveniently between the entrance porch in its original position midway along the south wall and the east end of the aisle. It now holds stained glass designed by Burne Jones and carried out by William Morris. It shows Christ with small children and a mother. Below is written 'Jesus called a little child unto Him'. It is dedicated 'To the Glory of God and in loving memory of George Hewitt Bostock who died April 22nd 1896 infant son of Samuel Bostock'.

The square-headed windows of two and three lights in the south aisle date from the 1883 restoration though possibly some of the original stone was re-used.

West Window of the South Aisle

This holds some of the original stone in the tracery but much was renewed in 1883. It consists of two lancets, one containing a stained glass figure of St. Peter and the other one of St. Stephen. The dedication is 'In Memory of Major General Sir Herbert Stewart K.C.B. born 30th June 1843, son of the Revd. Edward Stewart for 33 years Vicar of this Parish and Rector of Lainston'.

West Window in the Tower

This consists of two lancets in a quatrefoil, some of the tracery still remaining from the 15th century, above them the Stewart coat-of-arms. In the north lancet: St. Michael with spear and shield on pillars beside him 'Sancti Michael—Archiangelus'. In the south lancet: David holding the head of Goliath, on a pillar on his right 'David Pastor et Rex'. Below each figure is a small panel of glass with David and his sling and an old man, and St. Michael destroying the dragon. The dedication below is 'To the Glory of God and in memory of Major General Sir Herbert Stewart K.C.B., died February 16th 1885 from a wound received Jan 19th when in command of the column sent to relieve General Gordon at Khartoum. He was buried near the Gakdul Wells in the Banuda Desert'.

Monuments

North Wall of Chancel

The earliest memorial tablet commemorates the Rev. Edward Stewart (vicar, 1842–1875). A brass and marble tablet with a cross in brass and coloured enamel. Below is a rectangular panel surrounded with the text 'He maketh the storm a calm so that the waves thereof are still. Then are they glad because they are at rest. And so he bringeth them into the Haven where they would be, Ps. 29.30'.

On the panel is engraved Mr. Stewart's coat-of-arms and the inscription:

Revd. Edward Stewart
Born 9th October 1808
Died 21st March 1875
Vicar of this Parish 1842–1875

North Wall of the Lady Chapel

A green marble plaque with broken pediment superimposed in a grey marble base. In the broken pediment is a galleon in full sail and below it on a buff-coloured marble plaque

In Memory of
Helen Elizabeth
Born at Sparsholt 1849
Died in London 1926
For fifty-two years
The adored wife of

George Buckston Browne
FRCS
She never at any time
Brought grief upon me
Save when she died.

'Helen Elizabeth' had been a Miss Vaine, of one of the old Sparsholt families and met the young surgeon, later Sir George Buckston Browne, when he spent holidays in Sparsholt. He fell in love and married her and after her death many years later bought the cottages where her family had lived for generations and presented them to the National Trust to preserve them in perpetuity. They are now the property of the vicar and churchwardens for occupation by pensioners deserving well of the parish.

West Wall of the Nave

The war memorial was put up after the Second World War, commemorating 10 men who had died.

Entrance to Tower

A linen-fold panelling screen in dark oak was erected in 1941 in memory of Edward Cyril Raban (vicar, 1918–1941).

The Pulpit

This was given in memory of James Pern Fitt, Yeoman of Westley, died 20 Dec. 1878. Thirty years earlier he and his wife had presented a new altar to the church in the description of which he is described as 'Yeoman' of Westley. This altar is now in the Lady Chapel.

On the Wall by the Font

There is a good copy of a Murillo painting which itself hangs in the Prado, Madrid. It represents the Child Christ with the Boy John the Baptist to whom he holds out a drinking vessel. A lamb is near St. John. It was presented by Major Fawcett who lived in the parish.

Furnishings

The two Glastonbury chairs which stand in the chancel and at the entrance to the Lady Chapel were placed in the church by the Rev. Edward Stewart in November 1859 and August 1862.

The two large copper and brass candlesticks that stand in the sanctuary were given in memory of John and Eleanor Lewington.

In the 1880s, the Rev. Evelyn and Mrs. Heathcote presented to the church some fine wrought-iron candelabra made to their order in Venice. They cost £30 and still hang in the chancel and the nave. They later added lights for the pulpit, two lamp-stands on brackets at the west end, and additional lights at the bottom of the north aisle and one for the organ, all of Venetian work.

In 1888 Mr. and Mrs. Montague Cloete gave a tall candelabra for the lectern which matched the Venetian work. It was made in Winchester from designs provided by Mr. Heathcote, by Carter and Fabian.

The lectern stands on the wooden screw of a cider press. Both were found in the West Country by the Rev. Cyril Raban (vicar, 1918–1941).

The Organ—the Lady Chapel

In 1957 the organ was moved to its present position in the north-west corner of the church and the space left was made into the Lady Chapel separated from the chancel by the remains of the 18th-century gallery from the tower.

The Plate

The church plate belonging to Sparsholt consists of a flagon, a chalice with cover and a silver paten and almsdish. The chalice is a plain cup 7¼in. high and 3⅝in. in diameter at the top with no ornamentation except a pattern running round the base. On the cup is engraved in large letters 'The gift of William Masters M.A., Vicar of Sparsholt'. The hallmark is WB, the Lion, Leopard's head, the small Roman letter 'i' and the head of George IV. The cover is hallmarked in the same way, for the year 1826–7.

The flagon stands about 10½in. high and is about 5in. in diameter at the bottom, 3½in. at the top. On the bottom is engraved 'The gift of the Revd. Edward Stewart M.A. Vicar of the Church at Sparsholt 1869'. The hallmarks ᵂ·ᴾ·/ᴮ·ˢ·, the Crown, the Lion, the Roman letter capital 'A' and the head of Queen Victoria, indicate that it was made in Sheffield, 1868–9. On the side is engraved I.H.S. surrounded by a circle of flames and tongues of fire and rays.

The alms dish is 8½in. in diameter, with I.H.S., the Cross pattée, fitchée above and three nails below within a border of tongues of fire and rays in the centre and with an ornamental border. On the back is engraved 'The gift of Richard Barford. Vicar to the Church at Spershot 1766'. The hallmarks, Old English Capital 'L', the Leopard's head crowned, the Lion and ꜰ·ᴮ·/ꜰ·ᴄ· indicate 1766.

The paten is 6in. diameter. In a circle in the centre I.H.S. with a cross pattée, fitchée above and three nails below. The hallmarks are indistinct. The first is illegible, the second a Lion's head erased, the third a figure of Britannia, the fourth probably the capital letter 'R' indicating a date between 1696 and 1720. Below is scratched rather than engraved, 'Ex Dono Philippi Eyre'.

The church is very fortunate in being allowed to use the fine plate belonging to the church of St. Peter at Lainston which is now in ruins. This consists of a silver chalice and paten. The chalice is 7in. high with an engraved pattern running round the base. There is no inscription. The hallmarks are what appears to be a small 'l', the possible Lion, Leopard's head crowned, a large letter 'F'. The chalice is Elizabethan in design and is dated 1628.

The paten is plain solid silver 6¾in. in diameter engraved underneath, 'The gift of Jno Merrill Esq. to Lainston Church 1723'. Hallmarks are a crown with a star below and under that the letters L.A., under that a fleur-de-lis, a figure of Britannia, the Lion's head erased, Roman capital letter 'H'. The paten has a case of the same date, 1723. It is known to be by Paul de Lamerie who was goldsmith to Queen Anne, George I and George II.

The Bells

The bells of Sparsholt now number five. Four were made in 1742 by Robert Catlin, a very celebrated founder, successor, executor and residuary legatee to Samuel Knight who first founded at Reading, then in London and whose will was proved in 1739. Catlin's bells date from 1742 to 1751. At his death Thomas Swain took over the business.

In 1829, during the incumbency of the Rev. William Masters, one of the Catlin bells was sold, possibly because it was cracked beyond repair, for £19 7s. 6d. A new one, weighing 4cwt. 1qr., was put up by Thomas Mears. (His firm, later Mears and Stainbank, of Whitechapel, have for more than a century cared for the bells of Sparsholt church.) The cost of the work was £45 10s. 6d., less the price given for the metal of the old bell, making a charge on the parish of £26 3s. 0d.

This is the bell with the inscription

> T. Mears of London. Fecit 1829. Rev. W. Masters M.A. Vicar
> Thos. Foote and Thos. Mansbridge. Churchwardens.

Three out of the four original bells made by Robert Catlin bear the following inscriptions:

> Treble.—Tho I am but small I will be heard among you all. 1742.
> Four.—By adding to our notes weele raise and sound the good
> subscribers' praise. 1742.
> Tenor.—William Piper. Richard Lock.
> Churchwardens   R   Catlin.
> Fecit 1742.

In 1905 it was decided to add a fifth bell to the peal and also to re-cast the second and third of the old ring of four. The latter became the new fourth. The re-casting cost the parish £58, and the new bell, Third, cost £35 when hung. The total cost, including tuning, re-hanging and repairing the framework came to £150. The money to pay for all this was raised by subscriptions in the parish, some of the house-to-house lists of subscribers being still in existence. Mr. George Goater also generously offered to cart the bells from Winchester station for nothing.

The inscription on the new bell was:

Laudate Pueri Dominum
G. Dalhousie Ramsay.   Vicar
George Goater and Leonard Goater.   Churchwardens.

Something unfortunate seems to have happened to four, as it was again re-cast in 1914.

The tenor was re-cast in 1951, and the original inscription 'William Piper, Richard Lock. Churchwardens. R. Catlin. Fecit 1742' was repeated round the shoulder of the bell as before. On the waist of the bell was then added

Recast 1951
W. D. Maundrell, Vicar
D. Clapham.   S. S. Bostock.   Churchwardens.

The weights and measurements of the bells are as follows:

			cwt.	qrs.	lbs.
Tenor	35½in. diameter.	Weight ..	8	2	22
Second	27in. diameter.	Weight ..	4	0	14
Treble	25in. diameter.	Weight ..	3	3	0
Third			5	1	3
Fourth	31½in. diameter.	Weight ..	5	3	19

They still hang in the oak frame made for them when Robert Catlin cast the first bells in 1742. Though repaired at various times the old frame still sturdily supports the peal of five.

Chapter Seven

THE VICARS OF SPARSHOLT

FOR A LONG TIME after the Domesday Survey there could have been no resident priest in Sparsholt. The late Dr. Andrews, the Hampshire historian, thought the church would have been served by a Carmelite friar from Winchester.

The first mention by name of any vicar of Sparsholt is in 1204 (Curia Regis Roll 65, 1204) when there was a dispute over the advowson between two of the leading families of the district. Alan de Spersholte contested the right of John de Caritate to present an incumbent. It was proved, however, that the last priest, who had recently died, had been presented to the living by Godfrey de Caritate, father of John, after completion of the church which he had built.

This priest, **Robert**, must have been presented somewhere in the middle of the 12th century as a witness at the court of enquiry into the dispute declared that he had lived for more than eighty years, but whether as priest of Sparsholt for all that time is not clear.

The next mention is of **William**. A seal with an inscription round its perimeter was found early in this century at Andover. Its present whereabouts is unknown. The inscription is

S' WILL'I VICAR DE SPERSHOLTE'

The design shows St. Stephen, patron saint of the church, kneeling beneath the hand of God and praying for his murderers with drops of blood falling from his head. Behind him stands one of his assailants with a large stone held up in both hands; behind him another waits his turn to strike. Below all is the half figure of Vicar William praying.

36

The bronze seal is pointed oval in form with suspension loops at the back. The lettering dates it to 1240-1250. Two impressions of it are in the parish archives.

In 1297 one **Laurence**, described as vicar of the church of Spersholte was applying to the bishop for protection, but no reason is given.

In 1306 the Prioress and Convent of the Blessed Virgin and St. Mary Magdalene of Hartley Wyntney were mentioned in Bishop Henry Woodlock's register as 'parsons' of Sparsholt. By the context they had obviously failed to produce their crown dues for the year before and by order of the king (Edward I, 1272-1307) the bishop was ordered to raise the sum of £3 4s. 0d. from 'the benefice and goods [if any] of the Clerks', i.e., the resident priest. This meant the sequestration of the unfortunate man's possessions, and there must have been some resistance, as by July 1306 a writ was issued against the Archdeaconry of Winchester. By 1309 the sum payable had risen to £3 14s. 0d., though this may be a clerical error.

It is uncertain at what date the Convent of Hartley Wyntney were granted the patronage of the living of Sparsholt (*see* Chapter Five), but in the register of William of Wykeham (Bishop of Winchester, 1366-1404) there is a note that though the convent drew 25 marks from the parish and 16 marks from the vicarage the Priory of St. Swithun at Winchester retained the right to a 'pension' of 2s. per annum. These pensions were annual payments paid by churches connected with the monastery.

In 1333-1345 in the *Taxatio Spiritualis* the vicarage is assessed at 16 marks 21 shillings and 4 pence, plus the pension to St. Swithun's monastery of 8 shillings and 9 pence.

Richard of Astone was presented to the living on 16 March 1307, having come from Lincoln diocese. He must have been young as, according to Bishop Henry Woodlock's register, he was ordained sub-deacon at Highclere in 1307, and deacon at Breamore, when he was made vicar of Sparsholt, only five days before he was presented to the living. Two months later, on 20 May, he was ordained priest.

He seems to have fallen into trouble almost at once, as in the same register there is noted that on 20 June the bishop relaxed the sentence of excommunication and suspension passed on him for failing 'to pay the procuration at the time appointed'.

There is a gap in the list of the priests who served Sparsholt in the 14th century, and from Richard of Astone's induction in 1307 there is only one mention of the parish in all the registers of Bishops Sandale, Asserio, Stratford, Orlton and Edington, down to William of Wykeham. Orlton, who was bishop from 1333 to 1345, has mention of an institution at Westsparsolte during his episcopate, and the note that the presentation of the living was in the hands of the Prioress of Hartley Wyntney points to Westsparsolte being Sparsholt. No mention is made of the priest's name.

There may have been no resident priest at this time, Hartley Wyntney may have been too poor to pay a vicar, and a monk from St. Swithun's at Winchester probably celebrated Mass.

The preaching friars who, according to Chaucer, were sometimes disreputable, supplied much of the religious teaching of the time when there was no regular schooling, and the villages depended on them for news as well. The friars were often lenient with their penances for sins confessed and gave absolution more freely than perhaps did the resident priest, if there was one.

William of Wykeham, who became Bishop of Winchester in 1366, did not induct any priest at Sparsholt till 1376, so it is probable that **Thomas Gandean** had become vicar before 1366. He died in 1376 and was followed by **William Brounynge** who was inducted on 13 November 1376. This is the first mention of a well-known Sparsholt name, later to be spelled Browning.

In 1379, when desperate financial straits were seriously embarrassing the king (Richard II, 1377–1399), John of Gaunt assembled a parliament at Gloucester. This parliament annulled all former so-called voluntary grants of money from the people of England and substituted a graduated Poll Tax, strictly for national defence. Earls were to pay £4, barons £2.

The Bishop of Winchester (William of Wykeham) paid £4, and even the vicar of Sparsholt, William, presumably William Broungnye, was assessed at two shillings. His neighbour, Thomas, rector of Laneston (Lainston) paid the same.

The tax only produced £22,000, and was later repeated, thereby causing Wat Tyler's Rebellion, in an effort to raise £160,000.

John Bryghthrygh or Brightrich followed William Broun-ynge and was inducted on 4 October 1380. William of Wykeham's register gives the name of the parish as West-spereseholte. This may have been from its connection with the Forest of West Bere of which Deane in Sparsholt was one of the boundary hamlets. John Bryghthrygh exchanged almost immediately, on 16 October 1380 with John Louede or Love, who was rector of Little Kuybelle, or Kynewell (now Little Kimble) in the diocese of Lincoln. He lived for only a short time, and on his death William Wyndenhale was inducted on 24 October 1382. There are no more mentions of inductions to Sparsholt in William of Wykeham's register, and he was succeeded by Cardinal Beaufort in 1405. Beaufort was succeeded by Bishop Wayneflete (1447–1486). Bishop Courtenay (1487–1492) followed Wayneflete. Part II of Beaufort's register has vanished and in what remains there is no mention by name of any vicar of Sparsholt, nor is there any mention in the registers of Bishops Wayneflete and Courtenay.

Some time before 1485 John Willys, often referred to as Sir John Willys, had been appointed to Sparsholt and on his death Hugo Morecroft was inducted on 17 October 1485, presented by the Prioress and Convent of Hartley Wyntney. This is the first mention of 'first fruits' in connection with Sparsholt amounting to £16 19s. 2d. It was a proportion of the first year's income received from the parish by the incumbent and had to be paid before he took possession of his benefice or touched the profits of it.

In the Valuation of the Parishes (*Valor Ecclesiasticus*) of 1536 the benefice was valued at £16 10s. 2d. He appears to have been absent for a time, as in the Archdeacon's visitation book of 1520 Randall Crew, stated to be his curate, Richard Syms and John Ruston, churchwardens, declared to the archdeacon that the chancel of the church was in such a ruinous condition that divine service could not be heard there. This was also attested to by two other churchwardens, John Keriherd and Thomas More.

Hugo Morecroft was vicar for 53 years and apparently resigned in 1538. During his incumbency Hartley Wyntney Priory was dissolved by Thomas Cromwell in 1536 and the Great Tithe and Advowson of Sparsholt was granted to John Cooke 'the King's Servant' on 16 June 1539.

Richard Adams, according to Bishop Stephen Gardiner's register, was presented to the living 'on the resignation of Sir Hugo Morecroft' on 8 August 1539 by George, Thomas and Richard Poulet, Esquires. He was still vicar in 1551 and the churchwardens signing the visitation book have two well-known Sparsholt names, Richard Brownyng and John Loke. Richard Brownyng had signed the visitation book of 1527 as a parishioner. There was also a curate, at this time, one John Combe.

Richard Adams was deprived of his living in 1560 for refusing to take the Oath of Supremacy and possibly died that year. Twenty-three Hampshire clergy suffered deprivation in the early years of Elizabeth I's reign.

John Aberall, Abruall or Abrall came to Sparsholt some time in 1559–1560 after Richard Adams had been deprived of the living.

He compounded his first fruits on 19 October 1560, the sum due being £14 17s. 0d. (This remained the same sum, with a small increase of 2d. in Adam Airay's time [1621–1635], right up to William Purnell's incumbency in 1770.)

There is a mystery about John Aberall. He was certainly admitted to the living on the deprivation of Richard Adams, on 27 June 1560 presented by the Crown 'per proc John Williams. Clk.', and had the first fruits of it in 1561. He then paid two instalments of his commitments on his first fruits, £7 8s. 7d., but defaulted on the two payments for 1562. When summoned at the Hilary Term he pleaded ignorance of the demand being due but was evidently not believed and he was removed from the living. He may have been reinstated, as in 1563-4 he is quoted as still vicar of Sparsholt.

On the other hand, **Thomas Thurland** was presented to the living in his place by the Crown and compounded for his first fruits on 4 February 1563/4, and was inducted on the same day. He resigned in 1570.

Elizeus Hewghs or **Hewes** was admitted on 27 October 1570. Something is known of his character. In the Winchester Consistory Court Depositions, 1561-1602, there is the following:

Court Book 50, p. 284
13th October 1581.

Hyde v. Wayte

Elizeus Hewes, Vicar of Sparsholt, aged 37:

John Wayte and Thomas Sym met with this deponent in Winchester and told this deponent that the said Syms sold unto the said Wayte 20 sheep between St. Edward's Day and All Hallows Day in anno 1579 and they desired to compound with this deponent for the tithe of the wool of the said sheep due for the time between shear before and the sale of them. And this deponent, not knowing of the sale of the said sheep but by their relation, neither accustomed to receiving any such tithe for so short time, neither would demand anything of them. But the said Wayte and Syms, but especially the said Wayte, would needs compound with this deponent and give him somewhat, and so indeed they gave him six pence for the said tithe.

Elizeus Hewes was still living in 1591 and possibly lived on till 1609.

Richard Short, Shert or **Sherte** was admitted on 29 August 1609 on the death of the previous incumbent who is not named. He lived until 1628 and was succeeded by **Adam Airay** about whose date of institution there is diversity of opinion. Some authorities give it as 1621, others 1628. He compounded for his first fruits on 12 May 1628 and would not have been allowed to delay so long with this if he had been inducted in 1621, when in any case, his predecessor was still alive.

He spelt his name in a variety of ways: Airaye, Ayrey, Aray, Airey, and Ayray being some of the alternatives.

He is the first incumbent about whose education anything is known. He went to Queen's College, Oxford, 1604-5, and took his degree in October 1608, becoming M.A., 1611. He was ordained deacon in March 1611 and priest in 1612. He took a degree in divinity in 1619. Before coming to Sparsholt he was rector of Oakley, in Hampshire.

He did not stay long in Sparsholt, resigning almost immediately, perhaps in order to devote himself to his studies. A doctorate in divinity was conferred on him in 1637. After resigning the living of Sparsholt he became rector of Monks Sherborne in 1635.

He was later Principal of St. Edmund's Hall, Oxford and rector of Charlton in Otmore. He died on 15 December 1658 and is buried in the church at Charlton.

There is a mysterious James Airay who seems to have succeeded, or deputised for, Adam Airay, but both apparently resigned on 17 November 1635. Possibly James may have been a mistaken reading of Adam.

Edward Lane succeeded Airay, presented by the Crown, and was inducted on 19 January 1635/6. He continued vicar until his death at 80 in 1685.

He was born in 1605 and elected scholar of St. Paul's school, being one of the pupils of Alexander Gill the elder. On 4 July 1622 he was admitted to St. John's College, Cambridge, took his B.A. in 1625/6, and his M.A. in 1629. In March 1631 he was presented to the living of North Shoebury in Essex by the Crown, through the Lord Keeper, Thomas Coventry. He resigned this living on 28 January 1636 and was presented by the same patron to Sparsholt. He also became rector of Lainston from 30 November 1637.

According to the parish register, 1644 being a 'time of warre', Mr Lane was absent from Sparsholt, but was recommended by the Assembly of Divines to fill the sequestrated benefice of Sholden, Kent, on 27 February 1644/5.

When 'ye civil warre' was being waged in Hampshire the following note appears in the parish register: 'Because of ye absence of ye vicar in this time of trouble, there is no certaine account given of ye time when some few hereafter mentioned were baptised'. There is a similar note regarding burials. This gap was between 1644 and 1646. In 1645-6 there was a general ejection of Hampshire clergy from their livings owing to the staunch Royalist sympathies of the county and the city of Winchester (*V.C.H.,* Vol. II).

However, Mr. Lane was back in Sparsholt by 1646 as the death of his daughter Anne, the second of that name, is recorded in the register.

In 1667 he resigned the living of Lainston when accepting in plurality that of Nursling.

From 1638–1641 he spelt his name Llane. He was a prolific writer and, among other books, he wrote replies to Edward Hickeringill and Louis de Moulin, who held that probably not one in a million of the human race would be saved. Edward Lane's *Mercy Triumphant* (1680), was his reply. Against de Moulin's theory and Edward Hickeringill's he wrote *Du Moulin's Reflections Reverberated,* with an appendix entitled *Answer to 'The Naked Truth' The Second Part, by Edward Hickeringill.* Another of his writings was *Look unto Jesus,* which appeared in 1663.

To him Sparsholt owes the collecting together of the parish register in which for 50 years he made the entries. Something of his domestic joys and sorrows can be gathered from these entries.

He and his wife, Mary, had two sons and three daughters, all of whom died before him, as did his wife.

The eldest son, Edward, married and had one child, Jane, who was called after her mother, and died an infant of a few weeks in September 1660. Her father had himself died the previous May. Over his body there was a stone in the chancel (*see* Chapter five).

He was buried on 17 May 1660, and Jane on 27 September alongside her father.

The vicar's second son, Henry, born April 1639—he was baptised on 11 April—was a Wykehamist and a probationer scholar of New College, Oxford, but died at the age of 21 in October 1659, and was buried in the chancel of Sparsholt 'behind ye Reading Pew'. His brother and little niece were buried close by.

A daughter, Anna, was baptised on 6 November 1636 and died in December. Philaletheia was baptised on 17 February 1647 and lived to marry 'Robert Butler of Rumsey, -gentleman'.

The marriage took place at Sparsholt on 18 February 1668. She died at Mapperton, Almer, Dorset, on 18 December 1674 and was buried at Sparsholt on 23 December.

A third daughter, Anne, whose birth did not take place at Sparsholt, was buried here on 18 August 1646. She was probably born while the vicar was absent during the Civil War, possibly at Sholden.

Mrs. Mary Lane, his wife, was buried on 27 October 1669, and the old vicar himself died on 2 September 1685 and was buried under the altar; on the stone was carved:

> Under this Stone
> Expecting a happy
> Resurrection in Xt.
> Lieth . . . Revd. Edward Lane
> of the Flock for 50 years
> the faithful Pastor
> Come Lord Jesus.
> Died the 2nd September 1685
> In the 81st year of his age.

William Baker became vicar on 7 September 1685, presented by the Crown. Little is known of him except that he was not a graduate of Oxford or Cambridge. In the keeping of the registers he is distinguished from his predecessor by his strong and rather untidy handwriting.

Unlike his predecessor he was not rector of Lainston, but after Mr. Lane's death it appears from the register that people who died at Lainston were buried at Sparsholt. This is probably due to the very small burial ground at Lainston being reserved for the owner and his family.

The vicar often made notes upon the cause of death in an entry, such as 'July 13 1728 Richard Mislebrook, Junr. was buried. He hanged himself in ye widow Joliff's barn July 12th but by ye Jury att the Coroner's inquest being found non compos mentis he had Christian burial', and 'Sept. 28th 1725 John Rownin (or Bownin) a Coachman att Lainston servant to John Merrill Esq was buried, he was killed by a fall from a waggon coming from Winchester being soe bruised in his head by ye wheels that he dyed immediately on ye spott'. John Rownin, or Bownin, was buried close by the vestry door on the north side of the church, but his stone is now practically illegible. Another similar entry records the death of a boy who was killed when the horses ran away while he was ploughing.

One curious entry records the death of a man who seems to have had the same surname as his master. In September 1721 'Nathaniel Sidnam A servant to Colonel Sidnam and who dyed att Lainston was buried. Will. Baker, Vicar'.

Mr. Baker had one daughter, Jane, who married Edward Reeves of Hursley, died in July 1726, and was buried in the chancel at Sparsholt near her grandmother, another Jane.

William Baker died in 1731 and was buried within the sanctuary; the stone which covered him, together with that over his mother and daughter, were, like the Lane stones, removed to the tower in 1883.

Richard Barford succeeded Mr. Baker and was inducted on 13 December 1731, patron the Crown. The living at this time was worth about £100 per annum.

He went up to Exeter College, Oxford, at the age of 16 in 1723. He took his B.A. in 1727 and M.A. in 1729. He then became chaplain to Gertrude, Dowager Countess of Albemarle, to whom, perhaps, he owed his good fortune in the amount of benefices he managed to hold in plurality. In addition to being vicar of Sparsholt he was rector of Chilmore, Wiltshire, where he lived, and in 1736 was granted the living of South Newton, worth about £45 per year, and not far from Salisbury, but at the time stated quite falsely to be not more than ten miles distant from Sparsholt. In 1744 he was granted yet another living valued at about £200 per year, that of Wylye, Wiltshire.

At some time during his ministry he was made doctor of divinity as the St. James's, Piccadilly, register shows. He died in 1769 and was buried at St. James's, Piccadilly, on 22 November.

William Oldisworth Purnell, who had been curate at Sparsholt for four years, succeeded Richard Barford and was inducted on 13 January 1770, his patron the Crown. He was born in 1729 and educated at Winchester, becoming later a Fellow of the College, where he had rooms all the time he was at Sparsholt. He was comparatively wealthy, as after his death on 27 February 1775 the *Hampshire Chronicle* for 5 May reported the auction of his 'furniture' which included, besides his library and the contents of his cellar, 'cows, fat hogs and strong beer'.

He died while in residence at the college and was buried in the cloisters.

Richard Keate succeeded Purnell, presented by the Crown and being instituted on 28 February 1775. He was not inducted until 20 April and apparently was not resident in the parish. He had been rector of Chawton, Hampshire, and it is possible he retained this living and lived there. Certainly a curate, Nicholas Westcombe, was doing duty in 1783.

In 1794 Mr. Keate resigned the living at Sparsholt and became rector of Kings Nympton, Devon, from where in 1775 he was also elected headmaster of the Free Grammar School at Tiverton. He died at Kings Nympton at the age of 82 on 20 July 1812.

William Masters followed Keate and, presented by the Crown, was inducted on 25 March 1794. He was born in Winchester in 1749, was educated at the college and entered Merton College, Oxford, in 1767. He took his B.A., however, from Queen's College in 1776 and his M.A. in 1781. He became chaplain to the Bishop of Exeter and was inducted to the living at Paulersbury, Northamptonshire, in August 1776. Before coming to Sparsholt he had also been curate at Alresford for 21 years and did not come to live here till Michaelmas 1797. He held Sparsholt, valued then at £120 a year, together with Overton, Hampshire, which was valued at £70 per year and was supposed to be under 16 miles from Sparsholt. He was also granted the living of Shalborne, Berkshire, in 1796, worth £135 per year, and reported to be under 25 miles from Sparsholt. He then resigned the living of Overton.

All these pluralities were ended with the Pluralities Act of 1829.

William Masters lived till a great age and died in the vicarage (now Taylor's Mead) on 1 April 1842, aged ninety-three.

One or two slightly ribald anecdotes are told of him. It was his practice to bring his dog to church on Sundays and usually it lay peacefully at the foot of the pulpit while the vicar 'read his sermon'. One day another dog appeared in the church during the sermon and was immediately attacked by the vicar's dog. A fight ensued in the chancel. Mr. Masters left the pulpit, separated the dogs and returned, slightly flustered, to continue his sermon, but found that he had lost his place. Leaning over the pulpit he whispered loudly to the churchwarden who sat in the front pew, 'Goater, where was I?'

'Down in the chancel, sir, a-separating them dogs!' came the not very helpful reply.

Mr. Masters is also reported once absent-mindedly to have brought a Walter Scott novel instead of his book of sermons to the pulpit. He is said invariably to have sat while preaching.

A black slab to his memory and that of his wife used to lie over their tomb in the chancel but, as with those of the Lanes and the Bakers, it was removed to the tower floor in 1883.

Edward Stewart succeeded Mr. Masters on 30 June 1842. Born 9 October 1808, he was the eldest son of the Hon. Richard Stewart, fifth son of the 7th Earl of Galloway. He was educated at Eton, went to Oriel College, Oxford, in 1826, and took his B.A. in 1819, and his M.A. in 1834. That same year he was admitted a barrister of Lincoln's Inn, and subsequently became Member of Parliament for Wigtonshire and Private Secretary to Sir James Graham, M.P. Thus all set for a parliamentary career, what made him decide suddenly to take Holy Orders? The answer may perhaps be that he had come under the influence of the early Tractarians, i.e., Newman and Pusey, while at Oxford, and possibly association with the Fellows of his College may have changed the course of his life.

He was ordained deacon on 18 April 1841, and priest on 20 February 1842, not long before his admission to Sparsholt. At this time the living was, with the vicarage, worth £253 per year, the vicarial tithe being £300 7s. 8d. Patron, the Queen.

He married Louisa Anne, daughter of Mr. Herbert of Muckross, and they had three sons and six daughters. One of the sons became Major-General Sir Herbert Stewart, K.C.B., to whose memory two of the windows in Sparsholt church are dedicated.

Four of Mr. Stewart's other children are buried in the churchyard, just opposite and slightly east of the porch. One of them briefly followed his father into Holy Orders, and was curate for a year in Sparsholt.

The stones are engraved as follows:

> Sacred to the memory of Edward Horatio Stewart and Emily Susan Stewart, the son and daughter of the Revd. Edward Stewart, Vicar of this parish, and Louisa Anne, his wife. Edward died in his 4th year on the 14th, Emily died in her seventeenth year on the 18th June 1856. And were buried together in this grave.
>
> Blessed are the dead which die in the Lord.

> Sacred to the memory of Euphemia Stewart, daughter of the Revd. Edward Stewart, M.A., Vicar of this Parish. She was born on the 1st Feb. 1845 and after a prolonged illness died on the 9th April 1863.
>
> "Whom the Lord loveth He chasteneth."

> To the beloved memory of the Revd. William Antony Stewart, died July 31st 1883, aged 36 years. Charity never faileth.

Mr. Stewart evidently found the vicarage in poor repair and completely rebuilt it in 1843–4 at a cost of one thousand pounds. He did not come to live there until 10 May 1845.

After being vicar of Sparsholt for eight years he was also made rector of Lainston in 1850, the patron being Sir Frederick Harvey Bathurst, the owner of Lainston. Its value then was £24 10s. 6d. per year.

In 1869 he presented to Sparsholt church a silver flagon for use at Holy Communion which is still in use in the church.

In 1871 Mr. Stewart heard that Sir William Heathcote of Hursley Park, who owned the Great Tithe of Sparsholt, was about to sell it to the Ecclesiastical Commissioners. He therefore asked the Commissioners to increase the stipend of Sparsholt, generously offering to take no benefit himself, but to let the increase begin with the next incumbent. The Commissioners refused to consent. The Reverend Evelyn Heathcote, his successor, in his notes on the history of the parish, wrote sympathetically that 'Mr. Stewart had been burdened during almost his whole tenure of the Vicarage by having to pay an annual sum of Queen Anne's Bounty for the building of the Vicarage and to the Family Endowment Society for the Commutation of Tithes'.

Shortly before his death Mr. Stewart gave £50 invested in Consols to be applied to the benefit of the poor of the parish, and by his will he left a further £50 invested in the same way to be spent on distribution of clothing.

He was vicar for 33 years, and died at Brighton, where he is buried, at the age of sixty-seven.

A memorial tablet to him is on the north wall of the sanctuary. Underneath the Stewart arms is a cross on a marble plaque and the inscription

Revd. Edward Stewart
Born 9th October 1808
Died 21st March 1875
Vicar of Sparsholt
from 1842 to 1875

Evelyn Dawsonne Heathcote came to Sparsholt 23 June 1875. He was the fifth son of Sir William Heathcote, Bart., of Hursley Park, by his second wife, Selina, daughter of Evelyn J. Shirley, Esq., of Ettington, Warwickshire, and was born 11 November 1844. He went to Oriel College, Oxford, took his B.A. in 1867 and M.A. in 1870. He was ordained in 1869 and was curate of Dinton with Teffont Magna in Wiltshire till his appointment to Sparsholt, when he was at the same time made rector of Lainston.

He married on 19 December 1876 Grace, second daughter of James Hussey, Esq., of The Close, Salisbury; they had no children.

He took an immense interest in his parish and made exhaustive researches into its history, into the pedigrees of any family connected with Sparsholt and Lainston, listed the flora and fauna of the immediate district and (with the exception of the list of flora, which he unfortunately made by ticking off the plants on a printed catalogue that has not survived) he put all his notes into a black-covered foolscap notebook which is still in the possession of the parish, and is now stored in the County Record Office. He also put on record the full and accurate history of the notorious Elizabeth Chudleigh, who as Duchess of Kingston was tried by her peers and convicted of bigamy in 1776.

Mr. Heathcote was much beloved by his parishioners to whom he was a real father in God, and a companion, to whom all troubles could be taken with the assurance that if anything could be done to help he would do it. He would play cricket on Sunday afternoons with the young men, then when putting on his jacket after the game, he would say, 'Now, lads, I have been playing with you this afternoon; you can help me by coming to church this evening'. And they came.

He could be firm with a defaulter. Once one of the choir men, Mr. Bishop, failed to turn up and sent no message. The next Sunday when he arrived, he was asked by the vicar why he had not done so on the previous Sunday. 'Oh, well, sir, I wasn't feelin' too well and I thought I'd take a rest . . .' 'Oh, you did, did you?', replied the vicar. 'Well you'd better take your hat and coat and go home for another rest, then perhaps you'll be able to come next Sunday'.

Mr. Heathcote seldom wore a clerical collar as he considered himself part of the parish and did not want to seem to be set apart.

He made a complete survey of the parish and corrected several discrepancies in its history.

He resigned the living in 1893 for health reasons. After a period in London, in 1904 he moved to Winchester to an old house above the Weirs which had been the property of the Earle family. It stood immediately opposite the Old Chesil Rectory, but has long been demolished. He named it Hersent House, after a French refugee family which settled in Southampton in the 16th century with whom the Heathcotes had had business connections.

He died in 1906 and is buried in Winchester.

Francis Edward Ainger succeeded to the living. He was inducted on 8 February 1894 and became rector of Lainston at the same time. He went up to St. John's College, Cambridge, took his B.A. in 1882, and M.A. in 1887. He was ordained deacon in 1884, and priest in 1886. He was curate of Hemel Hempstead, 1884–1886, of Rothbury, Northumberland, 1886–1887, Newburn in the same county, 1887–1889, and of St. George, Callercoats, also in Northumberland, 1889–1891.

He married a Miss Douglas, daughter of Bishop Douglas.

In 1904 he exchanged livings with the Rev. Clifford Ramsay, becoming rector of St. John Evangelist, Jedburgh. He died at Jedburgh in 1905 and is buried there.

Clifford Dalhousie Ramsay was inducted on 29 March 1904 and became rector of Lainston at the same time. He was ordained deacon in 1878, priest in 1883, and went first as curate to St. Mark's, Victoria Docks, London. He then went to Shelsham from 1884 to 1887, when he became diocesan inspector for West Staffordshire 1887–1897. From 1888–1897 he was also Priest-in-Charge at Broughton, Staffordshire, and from 1897–1904 rector of St. John Evangelist, Jedburgh.

He was vicar of Sparsholt for 14 years and died in 1918.

Edward Cyril Raban succeeded Mr. Ramsay and was inducted on 15 August 1918, becoming rector of Lainston at the same time. He was educated at Clifton and became B.D. of London University in 1909. He was ordained deacon the same year and priest in 1910, his first curacy being at St. Peter's, Southsea, 1909–1912. He was curate of Holy Trinity, Guildford, 1914–1918. He was also a Member of Convocation.

In 1928 the two benefices of Sparsholt and Lainston were united, the values of them being respectively £244 5s. 0d. and £58 13s. 0d. Not till 1932 were the two civil parishes joined and a churchwarden of Lainston represents that parish on the Joint Parochial Church Council.

It was during Mr. Raban's incumbency that the Church Commissioners decided to sell the early Victorian vicarage of Sparsholt which had been built in 1843 in the time of

Mr. Stewart, and to build a more convenient house on land belonging to them on the eastern corner of Moorcourt Farm. The old vicarage was sold for £1,500, and in private hands was named Taylor's Mead, the old name of the adjacent meadow. Mr. Raban and his family moved into the new vicarage in July 1935.

He died in 1941 after being vicar for 23 years.

John Selwyn Sharp followed Mr. Raban and was inducted in 1942. He was born on 11 April 1882, son of the Rev. C. Sharp, vicar of Addlestone, Surrey. He was educated at St. John's School, Leatherhead, scholar of Jesus College, Cambridge, B.A., 1904; M.A., 1911. He went to the Bishop's Hostel, Farnham, in 1904, and was ordained deacon the same year. In 1907 he was ordained priest in Winchester Cathedral and was curate of Godalming, Surrey, 1906–1912. He became temporary chaplain to the forces 1916–1918, during his incumbency of Swavesey, Cambridgeshire, which lasted from 1912–1922. That year he became rector of Elvedon, Suffolk, and in 1927 transferred to Rattlesden in the same county. Five years later he transferred to the Oxford diocese and became vicar of Theale, Berkshire, 1932-1942. Transferring once more to the Diocese of Winchester he accepted the living of Sparsholt and Lainston in 1942.

He retired in 1950 and went to live in Winchester where he died in 1956. He is buried in Sparsholt churchyard.

Wolseley David Maundrell succeeded Mr. Sharp in 1950. He was born in 1920 and was educated at Radley College and New College, Oxford. He took his B.A. in 1941 and M.A. in 1945, obtaining a Theological Diploma in 1942. Ordained deacon in 1943 and priest in 1944, he became curate at Haslemere, Surrey, from 1943-49, and was domestic chaplain to the Bishop of Chichester from 1949-50. After six years in Sparsholt he transferred to the parish of Weeke, a suburb of Winchester.

In 1956 he was succeeded by **Edward Bannister**, who was at Lichfield Theological College in 1927, ordained deacon, 1929, and priest, 1930 at Manchester. He became curate of Patricroft, Manchester, 1929–1932 and was domestic chaplain to the Bishop of Bombay from 1932-1935. Curate of Christ Church, Moss Side, 1935–1937. Minor canon and sacrist of Winchester Cathedral, 1937–1938. Curate of Rickmansworth, 1938-1943. Perpetual curate of St. James, High Wych, 1943–1951. Minor canon and sacrist of Winchester Cathedral, 1951–1956. Vicar of Sparsholt, 1956. He retired in 1974 and was succeeded by

Edward David Cartwright, who became vicar of Sparsholt with Lainston, Archdeacon of Winchester, and honorary canon of Winchester Cathedral in December 1973. A Lincolnshire man and a Cambridge graduate (Selwyn College and Westcott House) he came to the Winchester diocese after 26 years as the incumbent of three parishes in and around Bristol. Before this he was a curate at Boston 'Stump' in Lincolnshire, and was ordained in that church in 1943. He was also secretary of the British Council of Churches, 1950–61, secretary of the Bristol Diocesan Conference and Synod, 1966–1973. For 17 years, 1956–73, he represented the Bristol clergy in the Church Assembly and General Synod. In 1973 and 1978 he was elected a Church Commissioner by the House of Clergy of the General Synod, and in 1978 became a member of the Board of Governors.

Curates of the Parish

1520	Randall Crew was curate to Hugo Morecroft.
1635	John Davis, or Davies, was curate to Adam Airay.
1745–1754	Charles Holloway was curate to Richard Barford.
1746-47	Richard Clarke was curate to Richard Barford.
1755	William Tourd was curate to Richard Barford.
1760–1766	Thomas Reid was curate to Richard Barford.
1765–1766	Henry Taylor may have been curate and did duty for Rev. W. O. Purnell during Richard Barford's incumbency.
1775	Phillip Williams may have been curate; he certainly did duty for the Rev. W. O. Purnell.
1776-1800	Nicholas Westcombe was curate to Richard Keate.
1796	Sam Rolleston Booth signed as curate *pro hac vice* during William Masters' incumbency.
1838–1839	C. H. Poore was curate to William Masters.
1839–1841	George Huntingford was curate to William Masters.

1853–1855 Charles Wickham was curate to Edward Stewart.

1855–1856 Edward Gunner was curate to Edward Stewart. Amongst the parish papers are still the papers licensing Mr. Gunner to be curate.

1876–1877 W. A. Stewart (son of the late Rev. Edward Stewart, vicar, 1842–1875) was curate to the Rev. Evelyn Heathcote. Mr. W. A. Stewart died, *aet* 36, in August 1883.

1879–1890 Arthur Young may have been curate-in-charge while the Rev. Evelyn Heathcote was absent for health reasons.

July 1901– W. A. R. Braybrooke was curate-in-charge during March 1902 Francis Ainger's incumbency.

Chapter Eight

THE REGISTERS

THE SPARSHOLT PARISH REGISTERS begin in 1607 for baptisms, 1630 for marriages, and 1628 for burials. Up to 1812 all these are combined in two books bound in heavy vellum covers, probably of the 18th century, measuring 13¼in. by 10in. Attached to the front end paper is the licence from the Head Distributor of Stamps for the County of Southampton, a certain G. Durnford, to 'Nicholas Westcomb, Curate, of the Vicarage Church of Sparsholt' to 'enter, write or cause to be entered and written, in the Register Book or Books of the Parish of Sparsholt all Entries of any Burial, Marriage, Birth or Christening without any Stamps or Marks affixed thereto, or thereupon; subject nevertheless to the Payment of the Duty imposed thereon by an Act, entitled "An Act for granting to His Majesty, a Stamp Duty on the Registry of Burials, Marriages, Births and Christenings" . . .'. This licence is dated 2 October 1783.

Nicholas Westcomb was at this time doing nearly all the duty for the absentee vicar, Richard Keate (1775-1794).

On the next leaf but one is a Memorandum by the Rev. Williams Masters (vicar, 1794-1842) of the census details for Sparsholt of 1801, 1811, 1821, 1831.

Both this leaf and the one partly occupied by the licence before it measure 13¼in. by 10in. to fit the covers. On the reverse side of the census details is a list of the vicars of the parish from the Rev. Richard Short (1609-1628), with various personal details about them, not all correct, down to the incumbency of the Rev. E. C. Raban (1918-1941).

There is evidence that a leaf has been removed; then come the 44 smaller vellum leaves, 7¾in. by 10in., which make up

Part I of the register. These are headed in the Rev. Edward
Lane's beautiful script 'Ecclesia et Memoraie Sacrum' with
below a note: 'A Register of as many Christenings, as are to
be found upon any Record since Mr. Short came to bee
Vicar heere in Sparsholt excepting ye two first which were
before his time'.

This, and a note of 1623, point certainly to Mr. Lane
having collected all previous records and transcribed them.
(He was vicar 1635–1685.)

The Rev. Richard Short came to Sparsholt in 1609. The
two baptisms before his time and the first recorded are:

> Thomas Godwin was baptised 20th April 1609.
>
> James, ye Sonne of Thomas Godwin was baptised ye 29th of
> July 1607.

Godwin is a name that appears frequently in the parish
down the following centuries, but the family are no longer
here.

Swiftly following the Godwins come family names once
well known in Sparsholt—Browning, Buxie, Lock, and
Blake—in baptisms occurring in 1612.

After 1623 a note states 'The rest of ye Names of such as
were christened in Mr. Short's time are either lost or els
forgotten to be putt into the old Register'. This is evidently
the early book referred to by Mr. Lane in his opening para-
graph, and which, having copied it, he probably destroyed.

Sometimes the vicars signed after an entry, or at the
bottom of a year's entries; others did not, and there seems
to have been no fixed rule. Edward Lane signed each entry.

Some entries have a touching charm:

> 1636. Will ye Sonne of a Wandering Woman called Jone Brown
> was baptised March 15th.
>
> 1637. Robert ye Sonne of a Wandering Musician born at Westley
> was baptised. April 30th.

After a baptism on 26 December 1644 is a note:

> Because of ye absence of the Vicar in this Time of Trouble
> there is no certain account given of ye Time when some persons
> hereafter mentioned were baptised.

Edward Lane was presumably evicted together with many other Hampshire clergy from this staunchly Royalist county, but by 1647 he was back in Sparsholt as he records the baptism on February 17th of his own daughter, Philaletheia.

The first baptism recorded as taking place at Lainston is entered in the Sparsholt register in 1649 the first of 19 baptismal entries, as well as four marriages, of Lainston people at Sparsholt and 13 burials, some at Lainston, some in Sparsholt churchyard. All these events, except the marriages, were definitely entered as taking place at Lainston or being of that parish, but yet are recorded in the Sparsholt book, thus giving ample proof that there never had been a Lainston register to be 'lost' at the trial of the Duchess of Kingston in 1776, other than that which that lady caused to be fabricated by the dying Thomas Amis (who had married her and Augustus Hervey) when she visited the old rector in 1759.

In 1666 a curious entry occurs:

> Alice ye daughter of John Waterman and Mary his Relict being ye wife of Marke Sims was Baptised March 1st.

In 1697 comes the first mention of the Vaine family, later on in the 18th century always to be described as 'otherwise Vaughn', with the baptism of Henry, son of Henry Vaine and Elizabeth his wife.

In 1720 comes the first mention of the Goater family, then spelt Gooter, and later Goter. This is the baptism of 'John, ye son of Thomas Gooter and Elizabeth his wife on June 26th'.

On 12 February 1708

> Jane ye daughter of Thomas Browning and Ruth his wife was privately baptised in ye night and on February 17th was brought to church to be publickly received into the congregation.

This entry starts a practice which soon became more frequent and cannot always have indicated a sickly infant.

The 17 leaves of baptismal entries end on 28 August 1724 when the Rev. William Baker (1685-1731) was making them.

There follows the register of marriages which begins in 1630. The writing is again Mr. Lane's, and his note before the heading 'Ecclesiac et Memoria Sacrum' is self-explanatory:

> A Register of the names of all those who have bene Married in Sparsholt since Mr. Airay, Principal of St. Edmund's Hall in Oxford came to bee Vicar here. No record being extant of any before.

*   *   *   *   *

Mr. Airay preceded Mr. Lane from 1628–1635.

A sign of the disruption caused by the 'Civil Warre' in village life is shown in the fact that from 1636–1659 there were only three marriages recorded. Under Cromwell and the Commonwealth only a civil marriage was permitted.

In 1668 the marriage of Mr. Lane's daughter Philaletheia to 'Robert Butler of Rumsey, Gent.' comes the first mention of marriage 'by Licent' and not by banns. Not till 1673 is there any mention of banns having been read.

Six leaves of marriages end in October 1737. Then comes a blank side of a leaf followed by

Baptisms 1724

The Reverend William Baker (1685–1731) was now vicar and his sprawling hand is large and on the whole easily legible, but it varies, as if he suffered from rheumatism in the hands; or possibly someone else may have deputised for him in filling in entries and signing his name which is invariably affixed to each entry.

There was a certain amount of illegitimacy in the parish but not so much in the early 18th century as in later years, but paternity was usually firmly indicated as in the following:

> Amy, daughter of Ann Witt, a single woman and Alexander Wade her master at Westley was baptised. March 10th 1727.

The final entry on these 4½ pages of baptisms is in a totally different writing and is unsigned.

Then follows a blank leaf after which comes Mr. Lane's writing again, starting the earliest record of burials in 1628.

Obviously copied from a much earlier book he fills in after 1635 the signature of Adam Airay and incidentally the name of another curate with the copied signature of one 'John Davis'.

Heading the record as usual 'Ecclesia et Sacrum Memoria', he prefaces the entries with a note:

A Register of ye Names of all such as been buryed in Sparsholt since Mr. Airay came to bee Vicar heere, and of all such as had been Buryed in Launston since Mr. Lane came to bee Rector there.

This last sentence seems further conclusive evidence that no special Lainston register ever existed till Elizabeth Chudleigh's hastily concocted one was made.

1637. A Wandering Musician's child who died at Westley was buried May 14th.
[This was no doubt the baby born there and baptised Robert on 30 April 1637.]

In the same year 'Mr. Peirce Roberts, Parson of Lainston, was buried at Sparsholt on September 24th' and in the following June his widow Dorothy was also buried here.

After an entry for 5 November 1644 comes a note in Edward Lane's writing:

In regard of ye Discontinuance of ye Vicar in this Time of Warre it cannot certainly bee knowne When some here under-written were Buried.

In 1646, however, Mr. Lane was in the parish and the second burial for that year was that of his own daughter Anne on 18 August.

In 1666 the Plague struck Sparsholt. Humphrey and Anne Bishop 'of Winton', evidently fleeing from the city's infection, brought it with them and died within nine days of each other at 'West Corner House, at Deane', and were there buried, being followed immediately by eight other inhabitants of Deane. Then Joseph Mour died at 'one of ye Parsonage Cottages by ye Parsonage Barn and was there buried August 3rd', followed in three days by his sister Anne. Four more members of the Mour family followed them and the village lost a total of 24 persons, all of them being buried where they died. One woman, Margaret, wife of Mark Sims, died of the 'Yellow Jaundice' and was buried in 'ye Church Litten' on 4 September as was another woman who died in childbed three days later.

There were cases of extreme longevity.

> Old Thomas Wade of Westley 100 years of age was buried July 20th.

Mr. Lane was using the old calendar reckoning in 1683–4 including January 1683 in 1682 and beginning 1683 with a burial in April.

Then the Rev. William Baker (1685–1731) begins his entries, one of his earliest sounding rather macabre.

> April 30th 1688. William Hobbs being very old was buried.

Curious items give glimpses of life in the early 18th century. When, perhaps invalided from the army, a man was making his way home, the following entry occurs:

> January 5th 1705. The Body of A Soldier who dyed at Killum Barne whose name was not known was Buried.

And evidence of inattention to dirt leading to blood poisoning:

> June 29th 1707. Richard Lock was Buried who dyed of a Prick in ye small of his Legg with Sheep Horn.

Evidently to be buried inside the church was not the privilege of important parishioners only, as in September 1708

> Mary Browne who dyed in childbed att Lainston then a servant to Mrs. Dawley of Lainston and wife to Richard Browne, then a servant to ye Deane of Winchester was Buried in ye middle of ye Parish Church at Sparsholt.

Accidents to adults and children were frequent. Jonas Hewett, a nine-year-old boy, fell down a well at Dene and was drowned, and Sarah, daughter of Edward Dyarway, was scalded to death 'in ye time of Brewing' in March 1726.

After 1737 come 4½ blank pages, then the Rev. Richard Barford (vicar 1731–1769) begins his record of

Baptisms 1731

His writing is very distinctive, scratchy and fairly clear, but does not often appear, and when it does his signature invariably follows. As he is known not to have been often resident one can but suppose he had a resident curate or a competent parish clerk. For the last four years of his incumbency he had a curate W. O. Purnell, who succeeded him as vicar.

At the beginning of the entries for 1735, inserted in very small writing between two other entries, is

> 1735. William, son of Richd. and Martha Barford Ap. 15.

Owing no doubt to no one person having charge of the register the next entries have only the day of the month written above them, then a line has been drawn below the entry of the baptism of John, son of John and Martha Browning, and beneath it a heading:

The Year 1735

Six entries follow, the last of them with 1 April after it. Below this comes

> April the 2nd. Seen and Allowed By us
> E. Hooker
> Thomas Barefoot.

They were presumably inspectors of registrations. Four more entries of baptisms follow and the entries end with one for November 1737.

This finishes the smaller of the two books in the vellum covers except that on the last page; if the book is turned top to bottom is a declaration in Mr. Lane's writing headed 'January 14. $\frac{63}{64}$ [1663-64]:

> It is now Agreed upon ye the Survyeours Office for Mending ye Highways shall be Annualy held by ye Parishioners according to ye Situation of their Dwelling Houses, Beginning with Mr. Hewet of Dane and Mrs. Wade of Westley
> > Edw Lane   Vicar
> > Will. Hewett
> > Tho. Blake.

By whom were nominated for ye yeere ensuing
William Hewett
Jane Wade, or her Deputy.

The next and larger book of 61 vellum leaves begins in 1737 with 'Christenings' in the incumbency of the Rev. Richard Barford (vicar 1731–1769).

Thomas Barefoot and Ric. Chal. Lobbe sign the bottom of the page of entries on 28 April 1739 as 'seen and allowed'.

Many of the baptisms at this time were untidily and sketchily recorded, often with no parental names; one entry is simply 'Goater baptised 1745'.

Private baptisms again became frequent after years of discontinuance, but there are no notes of the children being 'later publicly received into the congregation'. An entry may be as follows:

> 1767   Joseph Lee, son of a Gipsey privately baptised in Lainston House.

All this lack of care of the register is no doubt due to an absentee vicar and an indifferent curate.

Baptisms end at the foot of a page and in 1776, and the next page is devoted to

Marriages 1765

These end in 1781 and are followed by

Burials 1737

One curious entry is for 18 February 1766 with 'Charles Newby a Catholic at Dean. Directly to ye Grave and usual Service'.

At the end of the burial entries in 1769 is a note that 'November 15th 1769 died the Revd. Richard Barford M.A. vicar of this parish and Rector of Chilmark Wilts at which latter place he resided, and most probably was buried there. He was Vicar of Sparsholt 38 years. W. O. Purnell. M.A. succeeded'.

At this point it becomes necessary to turn the book upside-down, turn back six leaves and find

Marriages 1737

During all this time to 1765 Richard Barford was vicar and most of the work seems to have been done by a succession of curates. On three occasions—1756, 1757, 1758—the Rev. Thomas Amis, who at Lainston in 1744 married Elizabeth Chudleigh and Augustus Hervey, performed more orthodox marriages in Sparsholt and entered the facts in the register.

Marriage entries end in 1765 and it is necessary again to turn the book the other way up, turn over six leaves again to find

Baptisms 1777

On 2 May 1792 the first triplets, girls, ever recorded in the parish were baptised, born to Peter and Jenny Forder.

The 1783 baptisms are divided into two sections, a line being drawn after June and a small note put below 'since the Tax commenced'. Then entries for the latter part of the year follow. Inspections of the register took place every year in 1785, 1786 and 1787.

1794. William Masters (vicar 1794-1842) signs the beginning of the baptismal entries 25 March 1794.

1798. The Warner family are mentioned for the first time with the baptism of Elizabeth, daughter of James and Sarah Warner on 9 April.

Mr. Masters, who often appended notes regarding his entries, had absolutely no hesitation when entering a baptism of an illegitimate child in naming the reputed father.

1800. The Vaine family suddenly appear in entries as 'otherwise Vaughn'.

In 1806, 1807 and 1810 are three very strange entries having regard to the law regarding marriages of close relatives, when children were born and baptised, to 'John Butcher and Sarah, his Aunt'.

After May 1812 one turns over a leaf to find three entries then a note

Here endeth the Register of Baptisms from Henceforth a New
Register appointed by Act of Parliament, will be the sole authen-
tick Register of Baptisms.

> Dec. 31st 1812. William Masters. Vicar.

*   *   *   *   *

Turning back one leaf one finds

Marriages 1783–1795

During this time till 1794 Nicholas Westcombe was curate
and evidently from the registers did all the work for the
vicar, who was the Rev. Richard Keate and not often in the
parish.

One marriage entry, probably his first since becoming vicar
of Sparsholt, is entered by the Rev. William Masters in 1794
and he then signed as vicar and 'Curate of Alresford, Hants.'.

After 1795 begin

Burials 1769

In the recording of these for 1775 is:

Memorandum. About June or July 1775 died the Revd.
William Oldisworth Purnell M.A., Vicar of Sparsholt and Fellow
of Winchester College, and was buried in the cloister of the
College. aet 56. he was curate four years and Vicar six.

Again in 1794 comes a note that on

March 25th 1794 the Reverend Richard Keates M.A. Vicar of
this parish about nineteen years was presented to the Rectory of
Kings Nympton, in Devonshire. Wm. Masters M.A. succeeded to
the Vicarage of Sparsholt and had a Dispensation to hold the
Vicarage of Overton, Hants with Sparsholt.

In 1808 smallpox, a sporadic plague, visited the village,
and James Collis died of it at Winnall.

There was a great deal of infant mortality in the late 18th
and early 19th centuries; perhaps some of the causes are to
be found in an entry of the burial of

Ann Browning, widow, aet 75. Nourse and Midwife.

At 75 for her still to be acting as midwife, with the training, if any, of 50 years before, cannot have given a new-born
infant much hope of survival unless it was an exceptionally
strong child.

In 1810 there was another death from smallpox, again at
Winnall, where there may have been an isolation hospital.
This time it was Elizabeth, wife of Samuel Munday.

After the beginning of 1811 come nine leaves of marriages
then the final entry of burials for 1811 and those for 1812,
then Mr. Masters' note that there ended the register of
burials, worded as for baptisms.

Meanwhile the nine leaves before this contain marriages
for 1795 to 1812.

The last date on which a marriage was registered in this
book was 22 November 1812. Then Mr. Masters wrote his
valedictory message as for baptisms and burials and after
the two years of burials 1811–1812 three blank leaves finish
the book.

On the back end paper comes the following in the Rev.
Edward Stewart's writing:

> Sparsholt. 12 March 1846
> On this day there hath been placed in the Chancel a New
> Communion Table; the gift and offering of James Pern Fitt
> of Westley, Yeoman, and Ann his wife.
>
> E.S.

> Sparsholt 27 Nov. 1859.
> I placed this day in the Chancel one Glastonbury chair on the
> Epistle side of the Communion Table.
>
> E.S.

> On the 27th day of August 1862 I placed in the Chancel a
> second Glastonbury Chair.
>
> E.S.

*   *   *   *   *

From 1812 onwards by an Act of Parliament of George III
the registration of births, deaths and marriages was recorded
in separate books, printed for the purpose; there were to be
no more of the plain parchment or vellum leaves with room
for odd comments of the officiating priest.

The three registers in Sparsholt are handsome vellum-bound volumes, with beautiful hand-made paper leaves.

A further Act of Parliament was passed in 1823 to check clandestine marriages by insisting on banns being read publicly in church for three weeks before marriage could be performed, unless by special licence. The marriage register ends in November 1837, after entry No. 52, though there were 100 pages with room for 300 entries. The vellum-bound book similar to the three registers of 1812, stamped Banns of Marriage in Gothic lettering below the royal arms, starts in 1823 and is still in use.

The Marriage Registers from 1837

These are duplicates of each other and are still in use. They are bound in dark green morocco-type leather with brown soft leather spines and corners.

Andrew Vaine (36) when he married Elizabeth Smith (34) in February 1876 was described as 'Woodward', an ancient title stemming from Saxon days. The Vaines, a race of woodmen, probably knew more about the care of woodlands than anyone in the parish.

Another ancient profession is mentioned in the entry of the marriage of John Ridgman and Elizabeth Barber in 1833 when the bride's father's profession is described as being 'Postilion'.

Register of Baptisms from 1813

This begins in 1813 in accordance with the law and in the incumbency of William Masters (1794-1842). He always noted facts about his parishioners in the registers, and even now, though reduced to 1½in. square sections of the printed pages, he still managed to insert remarks in the 'Quality Trade or Profession of Father' section or in that of 'Names of Parents' or even that of 'Child's Christian Name'. He had no hesitation in entering in the case of an illegitimate child the name of the reputed father, or in listing the number of bastards a woman produced. Immorality, even when as in one case the man was married with eight children, was rife. Two men the vicar stigmatises as 'Vir lascivus' under the profession of each one.

A curious marriage, mentioned above, must have been that of John Butcher and 'his Aunt' Sarah. The vicar seems to have regarded it as slightly irregular as in each birth entry the father is named and before the mother's is 'his Aunt'. She died, aged 38, in 1821.

Some delightful old-fashioned names appear amongst the girls; such as Persis, Dorcas, Tryphena, Hannah and Philaletheia.

The Rev. Edward Stewart (vicar 1842-1875) records against the baptism of Jane, daughter of James and Elizabeth Dumper, on 27 October 1844 that she was the first to be baptised in 'the New Font'.

The register ends, fully used, in 1876, with 800 entries.

Register of Burials from 1813

This begins, as do the other two matching books, in 1813. From 1832 to December 1837 there are recorded sad entries of deaths of mental patients at 'The Lunatick Asylum' at Lainston House.

Mr. Stewart (vicar 1842–1875) was, like Mr. Masters before him, given to noting facts about his parishioners, though they were nearly all of a sympathetic nature. In the burials he mentions one man 'dropping dead coming up the hill to his house' (at Moor Court), and 'This poor little child was burnt to death'. 'Found drowned in Ashley Pond'; 'A pensioner of the 66th Regt'; 'Suddenly paralysed while at work in the fields he was taken to hospital and only survived the attack 21 hours'.

Mr. Heathcote (vicar 1875–1893) also noted in one case that a small girl 'had been choked by a piece of willow catkin which got into her windpipe'.

The book ends its 800 entries in February 1919.

The next register of burials begins in 1919 and kept inside the front cover is the form of service which was used on 8 November 1925 when the War Memorial Cross was dedicated. The cross was unveiled by Major-General Portal,

C.B., D.S.O., who also gave the address, after which the hymn 'For all the Saints who from their labours rest' was sung.

On a page facing the first entries is a list in Mr. Raban's writing (vicar 1918–1941) of charges for burials.

Baptisms 1876

This is a vellum-bound book, stamped in gold 'Sparsholt Parish 1876. Register of Baptisms' and the royal arms.

Though Sparsholt had had a fair number of twins down the centuries, only the second set of triplets is recorded in 1907, when Mrs. Sloper had three daughters in April 1907.

Lainston Marriage Register

The reason for the existence of this foolscap book bound in brown stamped soft leather with a red leather label on which is stamped in gold 'Marriage Register of Lainston', is given inside it.

Six blank leaves of paper water-marked with a fleur-de-lis begin the book, then on the page facing the first one with printed entry forms, is the following inscription in a flowing rather flowery handwriting:

> Whereas the Registry Book of this Rectory of Lainston in the County of Southampton, was some time since transmitted by the Revd. Stephen Kinchin, Rector thereof, to Elbrow Woodcock of Lincoln's Inn, London Esq. Sollicitor in the Cause respecting A Marriage, Questioned with the Duchess of Kingston, And application having been made by the said Rector to the said Elbrow Woodcock to return the same but without effect The same is supposed by us to be lost or mislaid, Whereupon We the Reverd. Robt. Bathurst, the Patron, and the said Stephen Kinchin have thought proper and deemed it requisite, That A New Register Book should be had for the life of the said Parish, As Witness our hands this thirty-first day of December in the Year of our Lord One Thousand seven hundred and seventy seven.
>
>   Sgd   Rt. Bathurst
>   Step. Kinchin Rector of Lainston.

Two marriage entries follow, that of Robert Thistlethwayte to Selina Frederick by special licence, 1 Jan. 1778, and Edward Pain to Anne Walldin (both of Lainston) by licence, 20 Aug. 1789.

The Rev. Robert Bathurst performed the first ceremony, evidently inscribing the new book only the day before the wedding, and the Rev. Samuel Gauntlett (who succeeded Mr. Kinchin as rector of Lainston in 1778) performed the second.

The remaining five leaves of 10 entries are blank.

It seems very odd that the 'Chudleigh' register was mislaid so soon. The trial of the Duchess of Kingston had taken place in April 1776 and yet, only 18 months later, it was impossible for the rightful keeper of it to obtain it from the solicitor, Elbrow Woodcock.

The Parish Clerks

The earliest mention of a parish clerk is a note in the burial register when

Edward Moore, clerk of the parish was buried 12 December 1635.
John More followed him, and after 50 years' service, was buried 16 October 1683.
Thomas More succeeded him and was buried 2 January 1693.
Richard Misselbrook was clerk in 1720.
William Goter was clerk in 1754 and died in December 1771.
John Cole was clerk from 1771 to 1788, but
John Goter acted as clerk from 1781 and thus began a family association with the post of parish clerk which lasted unbroken over three generations and 112 years. He was still at his post in 1813. As he died in June 1814 it is probable that he carried on till then.

John was followed by his son Robert who spelled his name Goater, as the family still does. Robert became clerk in 1818 and died aged 57 in November 1842.

John Goater, his son, seems to have been clerk for only a few months as he died in October 1843, and was succeeded by his brother, Robert Goater, who became clerk the same year and was still acting in the capacity 50 years later.

In 1893 Mr. Heathcote, the vicar, affectionately described him as 'an old-fashioned clerk of the old school with a clerk's voice and various mis-pronunciations peculiar to the race. He no longer sits in the chancel but now has a desk near the font at the bottom of the church, but even from that distant spot his voice is of an awakening character'.

He probably led the singing by blowing the opening note on the old bassoon, preserved in the church until it was stolen in 1978, which was not superseded by an organ until 1886.

Robert Avery, who was born on 3 Dec. 1872 and died aged 96 in October 1969, was verger for 40 years. To celebrate this record the parish gave him a party on 2 Dec. 1962 at which his children, grandchildren and great-grandchildren were present. He retired from the post only three weeks before his death.

Chapter Nine

THE OVERSEERS' ACCOUNT BOOK

A Rate made for the Relief of the Poor of
the Parish of Sparsholt in the
County of Southampton
for the year 1784

THE ABOVE is the inscription written at the beginning of one of the most interesting of the ancient documents that remain in the possession of the parish.

This immensely interesting record, now deposited in the Hampshire County Record Office, was in such a state of disintegration as to be impossible to consult before 1961, pieces of the old parchment being so rotten that they could only be picked up with forceps. A miraculous work of repair was done by the late Miss Forder, of Winchester, and now the book can easily be handled and read.

It is the day-to-day account book of the parish overseers whose function began in the reign of Elizabeth I. Their job was to look after the very poor, the old and infirm, and in some cases the orphans of the parish. They were also required to keep by them 'a convenient stock of flax, hemp, wool, thread, iron and other stuff to set the poor to work'. (Statute of 1601.) This was really an excellent way of making the very aged and poor feel that they were in some way supporting themselves.

The overseers not only looked after the living, paying a shilling a week to a woman looking after a sick person, but sometimes they paid for the shroud and whole funeral expenses of the destitute.

They were elected each year at the spring meeting of the Vestry of the parish. Legally the appointment was made by

71

the magistrates, but in most cases the parishes appointed the most suitable men. Two were usually elected; occasionally only one man took on this onerous job.

Money for poor relief was obtained by a rate, usually of 1s. or 6d. in the pound, levied on all parishioners and reckoned on rents payable by them. One year in order to produce the funds needed—usually between £120 and £150—no less than four separate rates of 1s. had to be levied. Defaulting over payments of the rate was probably frequent and there seems to have been no adequate means of enforcement.

Out of the money raised the overseers had also to pay the County rate of 3d. in the pound of the total raised by each parish. In 1791 Sparsholt paid £6 4s. 2d. and had a separate collector of the Land Tax (*Nomina Villarum* for the County of Southampton).

Among the list of ratepayers which starts each year's accounts were, in 1784, William White, who farmed Mare Court (Moorcourt) and paid 12s. 0d.; the Rev. Robert Bathurst, of Lainston, for his share of Crabwood, 1s. 6d.; Upper Deane, 4s.; Sparsholt parsonage, 8s.; and the vicarage, 4s. 'The Parsonage' may have been the glebe land or part of it.

Relief was distributed in money and in kind, weekly sums varying from 6d. to 4s. 6d. being paid to certain very old and needy men and women.

Another expenditure was payment for killing vermin, a small source of revenue to the village boys when 'sparrow-heds' were worth 2d. a dozen, hedgehogs and 'martin catts' 4d. each.

1784

[Poor relief was paid at 1s. to 2s. a week]

	s.	d.
A pair of Shoos for G. Crump	4	6
Spinning Tackell for Thos. Goater	13	0
A pair of shoes for Anne Newbolt	4	6
A coat and gown for Elizabeth Lovlock	10	6
James Gann for 5 weeks labour getting 50 faggots for the poor at 7/- per 50	10	0

John Goater and Joseph Strudwick for beving   ..   2   6
    [This may be droving or minding cattle]
Sparrowheds 3 dozen   6

[Names which appear in the book for this year, some of them still to be found in the parish are Avery, Browning (also spelt Brouning), Fielder, Goater, Foot, Dumper, Pern, and Buxey.]

1785

[Every year came an item for 'lining of the Poor Book', 4s., a fee for passing the accounts which were always duly scrutinised and signed by a Commissioner for Oaths.]

	s.	d.
William Butterley for tipping of shoes for the parish boyes [orphans in care of overseers]	1	6
Widow Browning and Elizabeth Studick 5 pints brandy	3	0
James Collis for 2 pare of shos	11	0
Thos. Foot for 3 Gints of Mutton	9	2
[He was the village butcher and this may have been provided for the poor of the parish]		
Paid to William Fifield for curing the itch of Livly's family	4	0
Sarah Lovlock for washing and mending John Lovlock	3	6
Mending the Poore Houses	5	8

[These four very primitive hovels of one room each, were thatched, with earth floors covered with straw and were kept for housing those who had nowhere to live and later for putting up vagrants who were being passed on to their own parishes. They were sold in 1843 the money being applied 'for the permanent advantage of the parish as the Poor Law Commissioners shall in that belief direct'. They stood, almost certainly, where the present Club Cottage stands.]

1786

	£	s.	d.
William White for bying Close for Mercy Williams his servant		12	9

	£	s.	d.
Mark Nores [who for years received relief at 1s. a week] for collecting six loads of stones [for road repairs]		1	0
Mark Nores for 16 loads of stone		5	0
John Goater for 55 faggots		8	4
John Wade for shoes for the poor	2	17	3

[At the end of this year disbursements had totalled £118 14s. 1d., against £122 7s. 0d. received in the rate.]

1787

[Robert Browning and Charles Fielder were elected overseers for the year.]

	s.	d.
The Gillett or Gillet family. Payments for the children varied at irregular but frequent intervals from 2s. to 1s.		
12 Ells of Doules and the Maken	17	0
Half bag of flour for Mrs. Buxey	16	8
Widow Hurst for Lainout Ed Abbott	2	0
His shroud	4	6
Swepen Chimbles for pore	1	0
Marten cats	1	0
30 lods of Stones picken	10	0
William Butterley a bill for the parish boyes shoes	1	10
48 sparrowheds		8
1 Doz of sparwood		2
Charity hovel [presumably for repairs]	4	0
Widow Abbot one gallon of beer	1	4
Expenses of swearing Cox to his parish	10	0
[This was the arrangement for passing vagrants on to their native parish for assistance]		

[This year 42 rates received totalled £143 0s 6d. Disbursements were £134 14s. 8½d.]

1788

	s.	d.
Lining the book	4	0
Young Peny shoos tiping		9
Cherrey Hurst in the Small Pox Hospital for her board of days	13	9

	s.	d.
A shroud	4	0
Bottle of Brandy	1	8
John Goater for the Bell [Tolling at funeral] and		
the Grave of Cherrie Hurst	2	6
John Gradidge for Cherrey Hurst's coffin	10	0
Ann Browning [Midwife] for Delivery the Travling		
Woman	5	0

[The County rates payable by the parish for this year came to £6 4s. 2d., and in the list of ratepayers it is stated that the rate for parish relief was fixed at 1s. in pound.]

1789

	£	s.	d.
William Mundy, the small pox	2	12	6
The Nurse for Couring Betsy Abbot's Back		5	6
2 pr stockings		4	0
Pair of Breetchies		7	6
Pound of Bacon			8
Gave a Man and a Woman		1	6
[Probably licensed beggars]			
Hedge hogs to John Gradidge		2	4
Half bag of Flower		9	0
Geave a man with a pass [a license]		1	0
14 gallon bread		6	0
Sweep of 3 chimbleys		1	4
6 hedgehogs		2	0

[No less than four separate rate of 1s. in the pound were levied this year in February, April, May and September.]

1790

	£	s.	d.
12 yds Dorulas for Jellets		16	0
6 Ells Dorulas for Beavis @ 10d.		9	6
Button and thread			3
2½ lining @ 7d..		2	6
Mrs. Jellets new shoes		6	9
Geave a man with a pass		1	0
Moving of John Mullons and expenses at Winchester		5	0

	£	s.	d.
Paid for Liquor at Church Recking		6	1½
[This entry occurs quite often]			
Beer, bacon and lard for Mullonses		2	2
[Lard was 6d a pound]			
Beer and mutton for ditto		3	0
Sweeping of chimneys for the Parish Housen		2	0
Paid for the Ringers		2	6
to John Goter. Due to him at Easter for Eating and Drinking		15	0
Bottel of Port Wine for Small Pox of Mary Moulens		2	0
Widow Mollins a bill for the Small Pox to Sutton	3	3	1
Widow Abot for caring Water to Mollins in the Small Pox		2	0
Henry Stevens' wife 29 days @ 1/- a day	1	9	0
[possibly nursing the Mollins family]			

[This year there were 15 recipients of Poor Relief at sums varying from 6d. to 3s. 8d. weekly.]

1791

	£	s.	d.
Mrs. James Coffin at Winton for James Fosbery Lodgin 38 weeks	1	18	0
Straw for the Poor House		12	0
Fagots for the Poor House		10	10
Thetching the Poor House		16	6
Shoes for Nickolas Browning		8	0
To Talmage's for inoculating Butterley's Family ..		2	0
Great Coat for Jem Wareham		10	0
2½ ells Dowles..		3	1½
Henry Vaine for killing a marten catt			6
Thecking Mark Norres house		2	0

[Dr. Corfe seems to have been the doctor for the village as a bill of his is paid £3 3s. 0d.

[There is a note that in addition to the rate collected £3 was subscribed for 'one bastard child Elizabeth Mundy'.

[That year the rates collected totalled £136 16s. 0d., the 'Disbursements' coming to £115 4s. 0d.

[For the second year running a farmer of the name of William Rufus was elected overseer.]

1792

[The Epiphany Sessions of 1792 agreed the charges for passing and conveying vagrants to their villages. To the constable or other officer when employed on this on foot the pay was up to 2s. per day. Conveying by horse, cart, on a turnpike or other road up to 3d. per mile. For conveying two or three vagrants up to 4d. per mile, more than six, 8d. per mile. Subsistence of vagrants in custody was rated at 4d. per day or 2d. for one night.]

	s.	d.
For expenses of taking up Sicman Rogers and keeping him hold one night. Paid for the receipt ..	7	2
Ann Newbolt for looking after Bett Browning [which she did for about three months] .. a week	1	0
Pint of Brandy to women who laid out Betty Browning	1	3
100 of bricks and 10 bushels hare for Poor House ..	7	0
Cart for carrying mortar from Slab Pond	1	0
To Bricklayer for work on parish houses	8	0
A bed matt. for Bett Livly	1	6
A bedstead for Nancy Browning	1	6
Bread and cheese for a poor woman		5

[The overseer also took people into Winchester 'to be examined', probably for smallpox, and also went in to buy a shroud for a child for 2s.]

1793

[This year there occurs the first mention of gin (the horrors of which were mostly confined to London and the big cities), when a pint of it, costing 1s., was bought for 'the wimen' who laid out William Gelet.

[The Dilidge Hutt, later the *Deluge* inn, now *The Rack and Manger* inn, is mentioned when the overseer paid 16s. for presumably the festivities on Easter Tuesday.

[A rather odd entry concerns the Fosbuary family when the overseer went to Laverstock for Fosbuary and seems to have put up the man and his son at his own house. Then Mr. Finch was paid 'for Fosbuary' £14 3s. 0d., and later the

overseer gave Fosbuary one shilling. Possibly the family were
locally born vagrants who had to be fetched from Laverstock,
but £14 3s. 0d. is a large sum for their transport.

[This year Mark Norries was paid 2s. for 'killing 4 marting
catts'].

1794

	s.	d.
A shroud	4	6
Licuer .:	1	0
2 gals beer for the small pox	2	0
Widow Mullins in the small pox		
2½ lbs. bacon @ 9d.	1	10½

Paid for Sharlot Wharam in the small pox @ 5 guineas
   a week

> [This can hardly have been the pest house
> charges and may have been for more expen-
> sive treatment. There must have been quite
> an epidemic of the disease as Gean Sturdges
> and Allin also caught it.]

30 doz. sparrows   2d a dozen

1795

[The shadow of the Press Gang evidently hung over the
parish this year. A peculiarly-spelt entry says that one seaman
was to be 'lined' out of three parishes, but £6 9s. 7½d. was
paid to the *Jestes of Peas* (Justices of the Peace) for '17 ought
of Sparsholt'. There was an arrangement whereby parishes
could buy immunity for their men, who were of course
badly needed on the land.]

1796

[The Livley family went down with the smallpox, Sam
among them; the overseers 'carried' Ann Livley to Winchester 'in the small pox' and paid 27s. for her removal to
the pest house. By 5 May she was up and about again,
however, and had a pair of shoes given her at 3s. 6d.

[Sam Livley's smallpox cost the parish two guineas.

[In June the overseer gave two men a mug of beer, 5d., for taking Hannah Light to the pest house in Orme Chase. This woman cost the parish quite a sum, as 'Barnet', perhaps the man in charge of the pest house, was paid £1 11s. 6d. for 1½ weeks; 14s. for four odd days 'Physick and Wine'; 'Cloathes' for her cost 5s. 6d; 'The making' was 1s. 8d. A final entry dismisses Hannah when the overseer paid 11s. for her 'aireing'—perhaps a final fumigation of herself or her house.]

The pest house charge of 21s. a week was for those days quite expensive and smallpox must have been a considerable drain on the parish funds, as in November Elizabeth Sturges's smallpox cost £3 15s. 6d., for Maria Holloway to be 'examined' the expenses were:

			s.	d.
Examination	6s. 0d. and		10	6
Expenses for the day			7	3½
Horse and cart			5	0
Corn and hay for ditto			1	0
The Overseer and Mr. Fitt to Winchester			4	2½
Spent on the woman's account			5	0

1797–1798

Four sailors with passes going through the village were given 2s. to buy them a meal. These passes were given them to establish their *bona fides* and get them a meal in the villages they passed through.

From now on the accounts show mostly just the weekly poor rate disbursed and more interesting notes disappear, but in February 1798 it cost 11s. 11d. in expenses for 'Swaring' Thomas Sutton to his parish. This to ensure that no one who was not a native of the village should become a liability to it.

In 1798 the first woman to be appointed overseer in Sparsholt was Mrs. Browning, who was elected with William White.

This year it was also agreed to gather two single rates of 1s. and one 6d. rate for the poor relief.

A mention of postal rates gives the cost of postage of a letter, the *cost to the recipient* being 4d. from the Isle of Wight.

1799

A small contribution to a Hampshire Militiaman's pay was evidently given by the parish. Dumper was paid 34s. 6d. for 23 weeks in the army.

Certain indigent people had their house rent, usually 1s. to 1s. 6d. a week, paid by the parish.

From this date the expenditure is almost only for the weekly payments to the very poor, and the handwriting of the overseer shows that a better-educated man is in charge.

Smallpox appeared again in May and was not to disappear entirely for many years.

1800

A man with a pass was given one shilling.

A bottle of brandy cost three shillings.

'Things at the shop' (this is the first mention of a village shop) cost 7s. 6d. for John Smith.

Sparrows and hedgehogs appear again: 2d. a dozen for the former and 4d. each for the latter.

Eggs were 1d. each and butter 1s. a pound.

Postal charges had slightly increased; a letter from Dumper in the Militia cost fivepence.

Chapter Ten

THE 19th-CENTURY CHURCH RATE BOOK

THERE IS A GAP of 18 years between the end of the 18th-century Rate Book and another, also still in the possession of the parish, which carries on the accounts from 1818 till 1897. It is not so detailed in its receipts and disbursements as the one preceding it. After 1875 it gives exact details of church offertories and on the opposite page how these were spent on incidental expenses for the church. This continues till 1897 within a few pages of the end of the book. These remaining 12 pages, starting from the back of the book, give Minutes of Vestry meetings, starting in March 1845 and ending in March 1875. From that date onwards the Vestry Minutes were recorded in another vellum-bound book.

The Vestry

Before County Councils and Rural District Councils took over the upkeep of the roads and the Parish Councils some of the civil administration of the villages, the annual Vestry meetings undertook a great deal of parish work.

The annual meeting was called in the early spring, though other special meetings could and often were convened at other times. The vicar took the chair, and those present included the parish clerk, the churchwardens, the sidesmen, the guardian of the poor, the overseers and the waywarden.

The Minute Book of Sparsholt which survives only goes back as far as 1876, but the Vestry was, of course, a far older institution. Side by side with the Manor Court which administered the affairs of the manor and was purely a civil court the Vestry dealt with everything pertaining to the religious life, and a good deal of the civil life of the parish.

In March 1876, when the vellum-bound Minute Book begins, the election of officials was the first business, as it was of every Vestry meeting. These consisted of:

The Parish Clerk, usually elected for life or till he resigned.

The Churchwardens. These were the Vicar's Warden and the Parish or People's, Warden. Their duties were connected with the repair of the church, provision of bread and wine for Holy Communion, and the care of the church furniture.

The Overseers. They had charge of the health of the poor of the parish, and one of their account books and several loose sheets and their expenses still exist. They were strictly speaking appointed by the Justices of the Peace, but in practice the parish Vestries were usually allowed to elect them.

The Guardian of the Poor. He administered the distribution of charitable sums paid to certain old and invalid villagers and represented the village at meetings of the Board of Guardians. He often doubled the appointment of overseer.

The Waywarden. He was responsible for the upkeep of the village roads. He collected stones, helped by people who earned a little money picking up flints off the fields, and filled in holes and ruts in the lanes and roads. When the state of the roads got too bad for village resources to pay for, he could and did report this to the Highway Authority. At a Vestry meeting in 1885 he was instructed to do this with regard to the road to Hursley, and Westley Lane.

In 1876 the Rev. Evelyn Heathcote had been vicar for less than a year, and Sparsholt owes the white vellum-covered Minute Book to Mr. Heathcote, whose love of recording the life of his parish has been very valuable. At this time Robert Goater was clerk. Brother, son and grandson of parish clerks, he became clerk in 1843 and in 1892 when Mr. Heathcote retired was still in the same post.

All the other officials were re-elected annually though they often retained their posts for many years.

In March 1876 George Smith and George Goater were respectively Vicar's Warden and Parish Warden; A. F.

Tyrwhitt Drake and W. Courtney the Overseers; and Mr. Fitt (almost certainly James Pern Fitt of Westley) was Guardian of the Poor and Waywarden. School managers were also elected. At this time it was decided to end the system of church rates and to pay for church expenses, repairs, etc., out of a monthly offering scheme.

From this date, though overseers, waywarden and guardians of the poor changed every year or two, the churchwardens remained the same for a long time.

In 1882 a piece of land (1 rood, 6 perches) was given by Sir Frederick Hervey Bathurst, of Lainston, as an addition to the churchyard, the fencing of which was to cost the parish £35 2s. 6d., or possibly more. It was agreed to raise the money for this and the legal fee by voluntary subscription.

At the 1883 meeting Mr. Heathcote revived the old office of sidesmen, two of which he said were needed to keep order in the church and churchyard. In 1885 it was discovered that the previously-elected guardian of the poor, Mr. Lipscomb, was not qualified to serve, so the vicar was elected and continued as guardian till the end of his incumbency to the benefit of the parish.

In 1886 a special meeting was called on 16 September to consider the preparation of a new valuation list for the parish which had been ordered by the Assessment Committee. A representative of the Ecclesiastical Commissioners attended, as the Commissioners were, and are, large landowners in the parish. They failed, however, to establish a claim to have the tithe rent reduced on Mere Court (Moorcourt) which was then in hand, by deduction of the tithe payable on the farm.

It is typical of Mr. Heathcote that he took upon himself the formidable task of checking every single acre and its rent charge throughout the parish. He found a considerable number of discrepancies in the rate book, with 215 acres unaccounted for, but by listing every person's property and ascertaining that these tallied with the 1846 tithe map he accounted for every perch in the parish of a total of 3,542 acres. The results of his work, beautifully tabulated, are to be found in his excellent handwriting in the pages of the Minute Book following the account of the meeting.

It is interesting to note that it was agreed without a single dissenting vote that shooting, when let separately from the land, should be rated at ninepence an acre. Mr. Scott Barnes, who was at that time the tenant of Lainston, seems to have shot over the entire parish, including Ball Down, Westley and Moorcourt, approximately 2,500 acres, rate at £93 4s. 6d.

By 1888 the village had acquired a policeman, the County Police having been started in 1856. He was to be instructed to 'apprehend mischievous village boys damaging the well'. This was a serious offence as damage to the well could endanger almost the entire village water supply.

In 1894 parish councils were formed, and this is indicated in the mention of election of officers of the Vestry of 1895 when the offices of overseer, guardian of the poor, and waywarden disappear from the Vestry records.

One of the last things done by the Vestry in the 19th century was the decision in 1899 to put up a tombstone for Robert Goater, over 50 years parish clerk, who had died in 1894.

Chapter Eleven

THE SCHOOL

PROBABLY the first form of school that started in Sparsholt was that of the craftsmen which had begun as a sort of child-minding by the more sedentary village craftsmen, such as bootmakers and carpenters, while the village mothers were working in the fields. To keep the children out of mischief the carpenter would make flat boards with handles, or a 'hornbook', the leaves made of horn slung on a leather thong, and paste on to them the letters of the alphabet. It kept the children quiet and taught them their letters. The craftsmen were paid ½d. a week per child.

From this arrangement developed the Dame's school, run by an older woman who had picked up some education. There were also the 'travelling pedagogues' who spent a month here and a month there giving the rudiments of schooling to the children. They were paid at the same rate as the craftsmen.

It is not known how long the Dame's school in Sparsholt had been going before the first Church school was founded in 1850. The very ancient Yew Tree Cottage in which the Dame's school was held was brick-and-timber built, with a heavily thatched roof and dated from at least the 16th century. It stood 50 yards from the church close to the edge of Woodman Lane leading to Ham Green and Hursley, till unnecessarily destroyed in 1974. This tiny building accommodated thirty to forty children.

Miss Everett, a niece of Mr. Scott Barnes, the tenant of Lainston House at the time, taught at that house those children whose parents could not afford the weekly three-pence per child to send them to the Dame's school.

In 1850 the Rev. Edward Stewart, the vicar, began planning a new school and persuaded Sir Frederick Hervey Bathurst, the owner of Lainston, to give a site which was legally secured to the vicar and churchwardens by a deed of gift dated 28 February 1850.

The building was to be brick and flint with a tiled roof, and a schoolroom 23ft. long, 16ft. wide, and 11ft. to the ceiling, giving six cubic feet to each of 60 children.

The cost was to be about £200, and the vicar obtained £65 from his parishioners, secured a promise of £5 from the Diocesan Board and £25 from the lord of the manor, Sir Frederick Hervey Bathurst. The National Society also subscribed £15.

Though elementary education did not become compulsory till 1880, by 1874 it had become popular, and the school building was once again too small.

At a meeting on 21 October 1874 it was decided to enlarge the school building in accordance with the requirements of the Education Department. A week later, 28 October, another meeting found it impossible to raise the money locally and the Education Department was informed. The parish was told that it would have to have a School Board. Disliking this, in January 1875, another meeting agreed to carry out the enlargement, to subscribe and raise the remainder by a rate, which seems to have been voluntary, rather on the lines of a guaranteed annual subscription. The vicar also made himself responsible for any deficit that might occur at the end of each year.

Mr. Stewart died in March 1875 and his no less energetic successor, the Rev. Evelyn Heathcote, took over the school plans. The cost was to be £205 5s. 8¼d., of which £131 5s. 0d. was raised by donations and grants, and £74 0s. 8¼d. by rate.

Apart from private people the following subscribed:

	£	s.	d.
Hampshire Diocesan Association	25	0	0
Ecclesiastical Commissioners	15	0	0
National Society	11	0	0
Dean and Chapter of Winchester	10	0	0
	£61	0	0

Maintenance of the school building was undertaken by a voluntary rate to which the Ecclesiastical Commissioners consented to contribute £3 per year. Books and fittings were to cost £45 1s. 6d.

There were 38 scholars on the books with an average attendance of thirty. This was a drop in numbers since the days of the Dame's school, and Miss Everett's class at Lainston, all the more strange as the population had risen in number and the original school building had been built to hold sixty. At that date possibly more space was allotted to each child.

Mrs. Bishop, the former school mistress, was retained as an assistant mistress at a salary of £10 a year. In November 1875 'a certificated school mistress from Salisbury Training School', Miss Elizabeth Barber, was engaged. She later married J. Ridgman, who was butler to Mr. Scott Barnes at Lainston, but remained headmistress for another 18 years at least, Mrs. Bishop assisting her.

By February 1876 the full expense of enlargement had come to £137 12s. 2½d., of which £66 5s. 0d. had been paid or promised, leaving £71 7s. 2½d. as a deficit, to cover which the Vestry agreed to make a sixpenny rate.

The upkeep was estimated at £35 per annum, of which £10 was to be subscribed privately and the rest by 'scholars' pence', threepence per week per child.

At that time the educational authority was the Committee of the Council of Education and with them the vicar had considerable trouble and correspondence. To begin with they refused to pass his plans, insisting that not only should there be windows in the south and east walls, but in the west one as well. The unfortunate children were to sit with their backs to the north wall so that the light was 'thrown on their faces' from the south window and the stipulated western window would also throw more light on the blackboard and the teacher's face. Mr. Stewart managed to prevent the western window being built. Having 'put aside' £32 as a grant, the committee made further stipulations. The building was to be built and finished and a certificate signed to the effect with the list of donors and subscribers. This offer had to be accepted within 14 days or it became null and void. Mr. Stewart may have wondered whether the trouble involved was going to be worth the £32. Better, perhaps, to pay it himself, and, in fact, he was prepared to pay £100 from his small stipend of £200 per year, as he stated when writing to Lord Lansdowne, an acquaintance of his father's and a member of the Privy Council, to seek his aid. Lord Lansdowne said he would do what he could, but that the rules of the Committee of the Council of Education were on the whole strict but just. He did not think the grant would be denied. From the Rev. Evelyn Heathcote's later notes it is evident that it was paid.

Fifty years later, in 1926, the boys of Claysemore School, then occupying Northwood Park, just across the parish border in Littleton, themselves enlarged the playground.

The school is now under the Education Authority, but as a Church school which the vicar visits three times a week to give religious instruction.

Chapter Twelve

CHARITIES

The Bricknell Charity

A sum of £14 was given some time in the 19th century by three donors, Messrs. Bricknell, Sims and Wade, for the distribution of bread to the poor of the parish, as far as the interest on the capital would extend. This was in the hands of the churchwardens who, at the spring Vestry meeting, would decide who amongst the needy parishioners should benefit.

The Smith Charity

In September 1864 Mr. George Smith paid £15 to the Charity Commissioners with which Consols £16 15s. 5d. were bought. The vicar and churchwardens were credited the following July with about ten shillings. At the Vestry meeting in March 1865 it was decided that two shillings' worth of bread each should be given to five old indigent parishioners. The first recipients were Widow Wallis and Betty Piper, Mrs. David Goater, John Gatehouse, and Charles Goater.

The benefits of both the Bricknell and Smith Charities seem to have been pooled and were distributed in bread on the festivals of St. Andrew and St. Thomas.

In 1866 and thereafter the charities were distributed in money instead of bread, two shillings to five different people on the same festivals.

The Stewart Charity

During his lifetime the Rev. Edward Stewart (vicar 1842–1875) made over £50 to the Charity Commissioners for the relief of the poor of the parish by an annual gift of clothing and by his will added a further £50. This was to be invested in the same stock as the previous sum and the annual interest 'to be distributed among such aged men and women of Sparsholt as the Vestry may from year to year direct'.

This last £50 the Trustees agreed to make over to the Charity Commissioners and that the interest should be applied to the relief of the poor by assisting them to buy clothing. The Charity was to be named The Stewart Charity for Clothing.

From Mr. Heathcote's notes it appears that the £50 left to the Charity Commissioners for investment had been specifically joined to the Bricknell and in July 1875 it was decided to keep the accounts of these two charities together. The interest was put into the Clothing Club and applied at the rate of 4s. per adult and 2s. per child annually.

Chapter Thirteen

THE WATER SUPPLY

UNTIL 1897 the chief village supply came from a well 247ft. deep, though popularly supposed to be 300ft. It was measured by the Rev. Evelyn Heathcote when cleaning operations were going on one year. Some houses, notably the vicarage, had their own wells, that of the vicarage being nine feet deeper than the village one. Deep as the wells were the supply sometimes failed in dry summers. When that happened a man had to drive a cart four miles into Winchester to draw water from the River Itchen. This happened in 1884.

The village well was originally covered with a wooden shed which housed the wooden wheel inside on which it was necessary for one or two people to walk treadmill fashion for about twenty minutes to draw a full bucket.

For the village memorial to Queen Victoria's Jubilee in 1897 everyone subscribed towards the present brick-built and and slate-roofed building close to the post office; this building replacing the shed and wheel, and having a tank in the roof for storage. A mechanical pump, worked for a time by a small windmill, drew up the water.

There is a legend often mentioned in old books on the district and even at one time meriting a letter in *The Times* some time after 1926, that one villager had long ago installed an ingenious system of raising the buckets from his well which was operated every time someone opened his gate. No one knows who this resourceful villager was, or where he lived.

Watley Cottage (Watley House) also had its own well as did the vanished house at the lower end of Home Lane,

Corner Cottage opposite the end of that lane and the *Plough* inn.

Mr. George Goater made a new one at Ham Green in the 1880s which was not a success, and there was a good one at New Barn, on Moorcourt. The others, listed by the Rev. Evelyn Heathcote with all his usual accuracy, were two at Westley, one at Ball Down, one at the *Rack and Manger* inn, two at Deane, one at Upper Deane (Deane House), and one at Crabwood.

Mr. Heathcote also noted that 'there was usually a man who made it his business to draw water and wheel it round to the cottagers who either cannot draw water for themselves or do not choose to do so and prefer paying a small amount per bucket. This applies only to the houses, about 34, which lie around the parish well'.

By 1895 feeling in the village began to react strongly against what must have been a hopelessly inadequate water supply. This was no doubt brought home more than ever severely during the summer of 1896 when water had once again to be carted from Weeke or from the Itchen at Winchester.

The Ecclesiastical Commissioners who owned Moorcourt Farm and other pieces of property in the village were approached by the committee appointed by the parish council to deal with plans for improving the supply. The Commissioners were not, however, willing to subscribe. The water supply at Moorcourt was, it appeared, sufficient for man and beast on the place, and this came from the very large pond, now filled in, which lay opposite the cottages and adjacent to the great barn (burnt down in October 1957). Apparently it would have been enough to supply the village itself as well 'if the water were not used for steam cultivation'. This was in the days when large-scale cultivations were carried out by steam engines.

The committee at first decided not to appeal to the District Council, but to raise the necessary funds by a rate on the parish. An estimate from Messrs. Dean and Smith was obtained for alternative schemes for raising the water from the 250ft. village well by a windmill, a steam engine, or an oil engine. These were to cost respectively:

£195 and 30s. maintenance for the first year.
£105 and £20 per annum maintenance.
£195 and £50 per annum maintenance.

All these schemes included the installation of a 6,000-gal. tank for water storage. Discussion dragged on over the years, the windmill scheme was abandoned and by 1898 an engine, it is uncertain from the correspondence of what type, was installed. The well house was entirely rebuilt at a cost of £60.

The water supply continued to be far from satisfactory and Mr. Samuel Bostock was a benefactor to the village, when finally, in 1908, some thirty years after the first correspondence began, he organised a pipe supply from Crabwood where a reservoir, filled by a pump from Littleton's vast underground supply sent a good pressure of water by gravity feed to the village. In 1957 the supply was connected with the Winchester main supply.

Health

Long before any organised health services the health of the village people was looked after by the parish officer who was appointed each year. In the 1870s there were two of these overseers. Several of the account sheets and the parish rates book of 1818–1875 survive and give an idea of treatments, the price of medicine and the rough-and-ready care meted out to the patients.

Charges at the Smallpox Hospital in Winchester were a guinea a week, and but for parish assistance would have been far beyond the means of most villagers. It was not till late in the century that Jenner discovered vaccination, thus increasing immunity and giving more chance of survival if the disease were contracted.

Anyone in Sparsholt requiring the doctor had to send a message to Winchester, as a surviving note indicates.

Dr. Crawford,
    Winton.

Sir, You are desired to attend on John Bounds of Sparsholt who is dangerous ill, please to come emeadly by desire of Mr. Thos. Fitt, Parish Officer, at Westley.

Dr. Crawford evidently paid two visits for which on the back of the note there is a receipt for two sums of two guineas.

In 1810–1815 a visit to a sick person cost 5s., and most items obtained from the doctor or the chemist in Winchester were pills of one sort or another which cost 2s. 6d. Others were:

								s.	d.
Sleeping pills	..	..	..	..	..	..	..	2	6
The Mixture	..	..	..	..	..	..	..	3	0
Lotion ..	..	..	..	..	..	..	..	5	0
Ointment .. .	..	..	..	..	..	..	..	2	6
Blister Ointment ..	..	..	..	..	..	..	..	4	6
Lint	..	..	..	..	..	..	..	2	0
The Boluses ..	..	..	..	..	..	..	..	4	0
Sago and Pearl Barley	..	..	..	..	..	..			6

In the parish officer's sheets for 1810–1811 and 1814–1815 the Warner family appear frequently.

'An emetic for Warner's son 6d.' This unfortunate lad had on the same day as his emetic a blister and a draught each costing one shilling. Spermaceti ointment was ordered on one visit, a pint of 'mixture', the next day, and four days later three leeches, besides a list of other medicaments.

Vermin Control

Another amenity undertaken by the churchwardens in the days long before pest control and county councils were heard of, was the killing of vermin, a continuation of the practice of the previous century. In the early years appear the following:

				s.	d.
1807	For Kilen of 7 Dusen of Sparrows	..	..	3	6
1808	4 dozen of sparrow heds ..	..	..	2	0
1809	Kilen of 12 Dusen of Sparrowes ..	..	..	6	0

and an undated bill states that Jessie Vain was paid 4d. each of killing six hedgehogs. It is difficult to see why hedgehogs were so disliked unless the old superstition still persisted that they milked the cows when the animals were lying out in the fields at night.

The Parish House

An item of 1808 states that for 'mending the thecken on the Parish house' 2s. 6d. per year was paid. This was for thatching the four hovels where vagrants and other homeless people were allowed to live temporarily.

Village Industries

Sparsholt never seems to have had any specific village industry. Most of the women probably worked on the farms on piece-work to help the family income. As late as the 1890s there was a much-beloved old woman, Mrs. Nellie Kirby, who every morning, as she had done from her earliest youth, used to go out to the fields to pick up stones. She was never seen without a spotlessly white apron covering her dress. The stones were there in plenty; the ubiquitous flints that constantly work their way up through the chalky soil. These were piled in heaps by the road sides of the fields and used to repair the roads.

For the men hurdle-making in the copses were kept up well into the 20th century, and the blacksmith, carpenter and boot and shoe repairer were always needed. But when in the later part of the 19th century roads became better kept and access to the towns easier, the harness-maker, furniture-maker and weaver gradually disappeared from country villages.

Sparsholt kept its boot and shoemaker till at least 1878, when *White's Gazetteer* shows that Mrs. Ann Bishop was the owner of the business. The blacksmith went on even later, Mr. Jeanes carrying on till his death in 1946 at the old smithy by Church Farm and latterly at the bungalow he built himself. This house is still called The Forge.

The Goater and Robinson families have long been associated with the building and carpentering trades in Sparsholt. George Goater established himself as a builder and carpenter when he bought the house at Ham Green which had been built somewhere about mid-century by Robert Avery's grandfather. This had been built of chalk blocks quarried nearby, and plastered over, on an acre of land he had bought for 1s. 6d. When at the old man's death he was discovered to be deeply in debt the house was sold and was ultimately bought by George Goater. It has long since been demolished.

The last of the craftsmen, Mr. Finch, though totally blind, carried on his cane-work and repairs in the little building that formerly housed the well machinery till he died in the 1960s.

*   *   *   *   *

Nonconformism

In 1865 the vicar, Mr. Stewart, discovered that the Methodists planned to buy the piece of land close to the parish well on which, till the fire of 1864, there had stood a cottage. He was always very quick to seize opportunities, and in this case felt it his duty to see that no rival place of worship, and so close to the church, should be set up in his parish. He succeeded in buying the land, of about four roods in extent, for £28. Later on it was sold to Thomas Goater and is that piece of ground between the well-house and the present post office.

Between 1893 and 1901, long after Mr. Stewart's death, a United Methodist chapel was built on the land where Wood Cottage now stands. This fell into disuse after some years, but another smaller chapel was later built on a site below the old Dame's School Cottage on the east side of the village street. Again, however, attendance fell to a negligible number and the building was converted into Chapel Cottage.

*   *   *   *   *

Smuggling

Some Sparsholt men supplemented their earnings with a little smuggling in the early part of the 19th century. In fact, it was said in Hampshire at that time that labourers could make so much money by these activities that they did not worry to find regular work. Robert Avery, who died aged 96 in October 1969, could remember his father telling him when he was a boy in the 1880s that he could well remember smuggling.

Brandy and wines were brought up from Southampton and probably other parts of the coast, through Hursley, and if danger from the Excise men was reported the barrels were dropped in a pit near the farm in Crabwood and later collected.

Also there was rumoured to be a cellar under the two cottages at the bottom of the hill at Deane which was used as a store, conveniently adjacent to the end of the deep lane running down from the ancient drove road of Ham Green along which the pack-ponies could have moved between the high hedges quite unseen from even a short distance away.

Very probably the smugglers used many of the ancient roads that abound in the district. If too risky to come through Hursley they could have come from the coast across the Test near Mottisfont along the pre-historic South Hampshire Ridgeway that runs near Braishfield, up through Parnholt Wood, past Farley Mount, and so along to join the Roman road close to Crabwood.

That the smugglers did not always get away with it is shown by a notice in the *Hampshire Chronicle* for 28 January, 1828.

> On Monday convictions took place before the Rev. E. Poulter and Dr. Newbolt of four Sparsholt residents, two for unlawfully having spirits in their possession and the others for selling beer without a licence, these fines varying from £25 to £12.10.0d. The extent of these illegal practices in Sparsholt and their ill effects on the labouring classes attracted the attention of the minister and the principal inhabitants and the Excise Officers were put in possession of the evidence which produced the convictions.

Chapter Fourteen

THE INNS

The Woodman

No one knows how old this ancient inn is. It was almost certainly the oldest inn in the village. It is described in a deed of 1756 as an 'ancient cottage'. From its position 2ft. from the edge of the road known as Woodman Lane, the main thoroughfare through the village, it was certainly built on part of the 'Lord's waste', probably by someone seizing his chance to encroach by the time-honoured method of depositing a few faggots on the ground beside the road. If he could do this unchecked he would from time to time add more faggots till a sizeable stack was made. Then with luck he could put up a small shed, till finally he had a cottage. If he could do all this unchecked he acquired an in-alienable right to the ground.

It is explicitly stated in an existing document of the Manor of Barton and Buddlesgate, dated 19 September 1745 that 'an ancient cottage built upon the Waste of the Lord with the garden thereunto adjoining containing by estimate 4 perches more or less with the Appurtenances in Sparsholt now in the possession of Henry Vaughan. TO HOLD the said premises with the appurtenances with the said Henry Vaughan son of William Vaughan, Elizabeth Lanston and Sarah Vaughan for the term of their lives . . . at the Will of the Lords according to the Custom of the said Manor yielding the years rent of 6d.' The entry fine was £1.1.8d.

Thus began a long tenancy by the Vaughan, later Vaine, family during which they seem to have had increasing

98

financial difficulties, raising mortgages and failing to pay
till in June 1857, they surrendered all estate into the hands
of the lords of the manor. There was by this time a brick
and timber dwelling house, thatched, with an adjacent stable
and piggery.

In 1867 it is described as *The Woodman* inn and a copy-
hold tenure. Ten years later when the Vaines were trying
to raise more money it is described as a 'beershop'. In 1880
it is *The Woodman* inn again, and H. Trimmer lends Andrew
Vaine £46 for a lease of it at £23 per annum. The surviving
deeds show an indescribable chaos of leases, mortgages,
debts and part payments.

In 1886, also, *vide* the Vestry minute book, the occupier
was B. Arnold. The rent was raised to £24 per annum.

In January 1886 the Ecclesiastical Commissioners (lords
of the manor) by Act of Parliament of 16 April 1861, sold
The Woodman inn to Sidney Greenwood Hill, brewers,
for £21. In 1887 they let the inn 'a public house' to John
Lewington (a well-known Sparsholt name) for one year
and from year to year at £21 in monthly instalments. Beer,
ales, wines and spirits were sold, the landlord supplying beer,
ales, and Porter. By 1893 the inn was yielding £40 per
annum rent.

In 1929 Sir George Buckston Browne had already bought
the two Vaine Cottages, home for many years of the Vaines
from whom came his wife Elizabeth. He wished to endow the
cottages as homes for two elderly couples of the village,
and bought *The Woodman* as a source of income for upkeep.
The plan did not succeed and he made over the inn to the
National Trust on 11 May 1929, and the Vaine Cottages
to the parish.

In 1973 *The Woodman* was de-licensed and sold as a
private house.

The Rack and Manger Inn

This inn was built some time before 1750 when it is mentioned in the Compotus Rolls as being 'lately erected'. It
was then called *The Swan*. It stands about 2½ miles from

the centre of Sparsholt at the extreme north-west corner
of the parish on the low-lying cross-roads Deluge Cross,
where the Crawley–Kings Somborne lane crosses the modern
A272 (Winchester–Salisbury). This was the old turnpike
between Winchester and Salisbury and had toll gates at
Weeke, Flowerdown, Lainston, and Balldown, the toll being
threepence per vehicle. The inn is mentioned in 1757 as
having a range of stables beside the road. In 1750 it was in
the possession of John Pascall with 40 luggs of land adjoining.
Rent six shillings per annum. Thomas Browning paid an
entry fine of £1 15s. 0d.

In 1751 John Merrill of Lainston surrendered the estate
'in the presence of John Dixon, deputy of William Pescod,
steward of the Manor during the lives of Thomas Browning,
his son Thomas and daughter Mary of messuage lately erected
called The Swan at Deluge Cross, in Sparsholt near Deluge
Pond in Crawley Parish, in possession of John Pascall with
40 luggs of land adjoining. Rent 6/- per annum. Entry fee
paid by Thomas Browning of £1.15.0d.'.

In August 1791 there is a licence to John Wade, William
Matthews and Millicent, his wife, late Millicent Wade, and
Thomas Deane to confirm lease by John Wade to Thomas
Deane of 'a messuage lately erected at Deluge Cross, Spar-
sholt, near Deluge Pond, Crawley parish, with 40 Luggs of
land adjoining being part of messuage and yardland called
Laceys, 1 toft of messuage and yard land in Sparsholt. Term
14 years from 25 March 1788.'

The Dilidge Hut is mentioned in the Sparsholt Overseers'
account book in 1793 when 16s. was paid for a supper to
be held there. This was almost certainly for the usual
festivities held on Easter Tuesday.

From the Compotus Rolls comes a list of occupiers:

    1783   William Matthews, late Wade.
    1799   Charles Avery.
    1809   Charles Wade Derby.
    1856   William Ings, Walter Hoare Ings and Thomas Ings.

An indenture of 2 November 1821 states that William
Matthews of Winchester, 'one of the lay canons of the
Cathedral church' leased the inn to William Ings of Sparsholt

on a 21-year lease at a rent of £21 per annum as an Ale House for sale of ale or beer and Spirituous Liquors'. The owner agreed to spend 30s. a year on 'most necessary and substantial repairs to the messuage' while the occupier kept the inn and its building in repair.

It is described as 'now known as The Rack and Manger on the extreme western corner of the parish which before had also been known as The Deluge'.

An entry in the Compotus Rolls for 1837 still describes it as 'lately erected, built at Deluge Cross with 40 luggs of land adjoining now set off with metes and bounds being part of a messuage and yardland called Laceys and toft of a part of a messuage and yardland in Sparsholt with 40 luggs of land lately enclosed near the Turnpike Road adjoining the same premises'.

In 1886 according to the Sparsholt Vestry Minute Book, the occupier was Hampshire, whose rent was reduced to £12 per annum.

Mrs. Jane Bucksey was the occupier in 1878 and in *White's Gazetteer* is described as a victualler.

The reason for an inn being built in this isolated spot was undoubtedly the frequent need for horses to haul out wagons, coaches and carriages from the bog that winter storms made of this low-lying cross-roads at the bottom of two steep hills to east and west. Diagonally opposite was Deluge Pond, fed by the overflow from Crawley village pond, half a mile north, which added to the floods. It is only a few years ago that a range of stables in the inn yard was demolished.

The Plough Inn

Nothing is known about the origin of this inn which lies conveniently at the entry to the village on the lane up from the A272. The present two-storey house is probably early 19th-century, and built on the foundations of a much earlier building. Up to a few years ago it had a good range of out-buildings which may show that it originated as a small-holding of about one-and-a-half acres, but being conveniently close to the side of the road the occupier decided to apply for a licence. There was also originally a pond beside the old yew tree on the edge of the road, which though now filled in still floods the low-lying part of the road after heavy rain. Apart from the need for horses to haul out carriages and carts the occupier would have found it convenient to supply refreshment to the drivers and passengers.

It was re-assessed in 1886, the rent being fixed at £14 8s. 0d. per annum.

Chapter Fifteen

THE FORMING OF THE VILLAGE

STANDING ON THE KNOLL at the centre of the village where Westley Lane ends in the main street is the church, undoubtedly the oldest building in Sparsholt (see chapter on The Church). Opposite, on the extreme edge of the south corner of the junction of lane and street, stands a very small building, Church Cottage, reputed to be the oldest house in the village. It may well be that as it is certainly the smallest, standing tucked into a small triangular space carved out of the high-rising chalkland behind which rises to roof level. The gate opens on to a slip of garden a yard wide at the corner of the road junction with a small yard at the back. No one knows the date of the building. Till 1925 it was thatched. It is rough-cast over brick in front and over chalk at the back. It might have housed the first vicar, probably a celibate.

Opposite the junction of lane and street stands the house 'Opposite the Church', a 16th-century brick and timber structure which was originally the house of the parish clerk and was known in 1895 as 'The Old Clerk's Cottage'. Over the years it has been much altered and its thatched roof replaced with tiles. It has a cellar and a well, and a yew tree approximately 400 years old.

The village street, Woodman Lane, leads south and immediately below Church Cottage on the same side of the road is the house called Club Cottage which is a recent conversion of the 18th-century Club Cottages, a pair made out of the original 'Parish House' which housed vagrants or people moving through with passes to their native villages, or soldiers with passes on their way home after service. The

103

18th-century overseer's book has several mentions of it with one entry of payment for its 'thecken' or thatch.

Almost opposite is the entrance to a bungalow built by the last Sparsholt blacksmith, Mr. Jeanes, for his retirement before the 1914–18 war. He brought his ancient anvil with him and it still stands in the garden.

On the same side of the street, slightly lower down, stood until 1968 a very ancient thatched, brick and timber cottage, Yew Tree Cottage, which dated certainly from at least the 16th century, possibly from before. It housed the original Dame's school and is reputed to have held 40 children. As a school it was not superseded till 1870. A modern house now occupies the site.

Further down the lane in the narrowest part and on the west side stand two 16th-17th-century cottages, joined together, but differing in architecture, Rudgewick and Wheatlands. Both were originally thatched and of brick and timber. Rudgewick was tiled with concrete tiles in about 1925.

A few yards below on the east side of the lane is The Woodman, now a private house and de-licensed in 1973 (see The Inns chapter). Heavily thatched with whitewashed brick walls it stands only three feet from the edge of the narrow lane.

Immediately beyond The Woodman is the entrance to the county council housing estate, started in 1939, which now comprises 44 houses, four bungalows in Woodman Close, and eight flats in the adjacent Stockwell Place. These stand on part of the original common fields of Sparsholt which covered about 30 acres. Beyond the entrance to Woodman Close the county council built four more cottages in 1926 and aptly named them Sparsholt Fields, as they stand on the edge of the old common fields.

A modern cottage and a bungalow stand beyond and here the main part of the village ends with the fields of Moorcourt Farm on the west side of the road.

Further down the lane lies Ham Green, part of the waste of the manor, crossed by the Ox Drove coming in from the west (see Footpaths). Ham Green House, a Victorian building, stands on the western edge of the Green and opposite is a fairly ancient pair of cottages of brick and timber construction, now one house.

Robert Avery, who died in 1969, aged 94, remembered that in the early 1880s his father bought from the lords of the manor one acre of Ham Green for 1s. 6d., and built on it a cottage of chalk blocks a few yards in from the edge of the road where the Ox Drove crossed to Ham Green. This has unfortunately long since disappeared.

Ham Green and Ox Drove continue east as a wide green track, partly overgrown with blackthorn, but still in use as a bridle path (see Footpaths, etc.).

At Ham Green the village ends and the lane continues through Crabwood to Hursley.

Starting west from the church Westley Lane runs past several old houses. Immediately after the modern Clareholme, standing beside the churchyard, come the Vaine Cottages, for many years occupied by members of the Vaine family and bought in 1926 by Sir George Buckston Browne in memory of his wife, Elizabeth Vaine. He presented them to Sparsholt parish for occupation, rent free, by parishioners who deserved well of the parish. The Vaine Cottages date from the 17th century and are of brick, tile hung, and thatched.

Opposite them stands Halston House, once two cottages dating from 1636. It is of brick with timber framing and is thatched. It was converted into one house late in the 19th century.

Just beyond stands the White House and its great thatched barn. Built of brick, whitewashed, with cellar, the house was a farmhouse and in the late 19th century was occupied by John Lewington, who was also coach driver to the judge at the Quarter Sessions. He stabled the horses and the coach in the thatched barn which is 70ft. long and dates from the 15th to 16th centuries.

Opposite the White House is the entrance to Lambourne Close, a small county council housing estate of four houses, built in 1926.

A few yards further on is a small green a few square yards in extent, beside which stand two modern houses and a conversion of two cottages, Wood Cottage. This was briefly in the 19th century a nonconformist chapel, became again two cottages, and is now a private house. It dates, probably, from early 19th century, but may be older.

Off the little green opens a short approach to The Lodge which is Victorian, brick built and originally of one storey. A second storey was added in the 1920s.

Fifty yards further down Westley Lane stands on the left a brick-and-timber-framed thatched house, dating from the 17th century, The Thatched Cottage, originally two houses. It was enlarged to the west in 1967.

Beyond this a lane branches off towards Moorcourt. The present Victorian house almost certainly occupies the site of the original manor house of Moorcourt (or Morecourt). A very ancient great barn originally stood near the house but was burnt down in October 1957 and completely destroyed. The large farm pond on which the village people used to skate in hard winters, and which might have saved the barn, had over the years been allowed to silt up and is now only traceable as a hollow in the ground.

A lane leads past the house downhill to New Barn Farm and the Ox Drove.

From the lane junction at The Thatched House Westley Lane runs winding for three-quarters of a mile to the entrance to Westley Farm, now the Hampshire College of Agriculture. It was the manor house of Westley Manor and is Georgian, of brick, and wholly delightful. Known to have been in existence in 1845 it is clearly much older. Nearby is a flint and brick stable dated by a plaque on the end gable J.P.F. 1871/ (J.P.F. was James Pern Fitt, the occupier). There are dovecote holes in the end gable and along the south-west wall. None of the other buildings survive as a result of two disastrous fires in the middle 19th century.

Beyond the entrance to Westley stands Garstons, built between 1845 and 1875 with flint chiselling in panels on the original structure. This has been added on to twice since 1900. It has two magnificent oaks in the paddock.

Returning to the green beside the Lodge gate Home Lane turns north and runs past a few modern cottages and houses to The Cottage. Originally two thatched cottages of about 17th-century date, it is timber-framed with brick infilling. It was converted to one house in the 1920s.

Just beyond on the opposite side of the lane is Pies Cottage which is possibly the second oldest habitation in Sparsholt. There is a legend that it has Saxon foundations. However that may be it was until 1977 a lovely example of 15th-century brick and timber-framed construction with thatched roof. There was also a deep circular brick-lined pool between the gate and the door which may have been a small converted horse pond. Pies was originally two very small cottages, later turned into one. Each had its own well. Unfortunately, it has now been doubled in size and the walls raised by about 6ft. so that it no longer has any interest or beauty. The pool has been filled in.

At the bottom of Home Lane where it joins Watley Lane stands Corner Cottage, 18th century, thatched and with chequer brick walls.

To the left a few yards further on is the entrance to Watley House and Farm. At this entrance stands the 18th-century thatched brick Watley Cottage. A little further up the lane on the left is Watley House, originally Watley Farmhouse. It has two storeys and an attic and is of colour-washed brick with an old tiled roof. It is 18th century.

Locks Lane, a bridle path, runs past it and the modern Watley Farm and comes out into Westley Lane in about a quarter of a mile, passing the modern cricket ground.

The village street runs from the church northwards and crosses the village green on which stands the Memorial Hall, built after the 1914–18 war, with the school beyond. On the opposite side of the road is the memorial to Sparsholt men who died in the two World Wars. The Street passes the little building housing the old village well, 247ft. deep. The well-house was built by public subscription in 1897 to celebrate Queen Victoria's Jubilee.

The post office and village shop was rebuilt after a fire which demolished several adjacent cottages in 1864.

Just beyond the post office on the opposite side of the road stands Taylor's Mead, originally the vicarage, a two-storey brick house with slate roof, rebuilt in 1843 when very dilapidated, and is probably only 18th century in origin.

About one hundred yards further north on the east side is Manor Cottage, of unknown date, probably 19th century on much older foundations. In the cellar is a pointed arch, blocked up, of unknown date.

The modern manor house (1929) stands beyond on the right, and a little further on is *The Plough* inn (see The Inns).

Continuing north the lane comes shortly to the top of Dean Lane opposite which turns off the Back Drive to Lainston House. At this crossing of lanes the ghost of a monk in habit and cowl has been seen at various times. He has also been seen in the Manor Cottage. Nothing more is known of this apparition.

The village lane leads on past the turning to Deane, passing Deane House on the right, a two-storeyed building dating from 1786. It has lead lion-head masks on the roof guttering. The gate lodge at the bottom of the hill at the end of the Drive is 17th-century and stands on foundations of early farm buildings. The lane goes on to its junction with A272.

Turning down Deane Lane, opposite Lainston Back Drive, this very narrow, deeply-sunk lane passes Dean Hill Cottage, a two-storeyed brick building of unknown date and originally two cottages. In digging a new cesspit during alterations in 1965 an 11th-century cooking pot was found.

At the bottom of the hill the lane turns sharply left into the tiny hamlet of Deane, a group of very ancient cottages and farm houses lining one side of the road. At the foot of the hill the only house on the right is Barn Cottage, 16th–17th century, originally a farmhouse, of brick, timber-framed and thatched. It was added to in 1968.

Opposite on the corner, stands Apple Tree Cottage, two storeys and of brick, with a cellar. The reputed inner secret cellar in which 18th- and 19th-century smugglers hid contraband wines and spirits, when on the run from Excise officers through Crabwood and Ham Green, has never been discovered in spite of much searching.

Next door is the Old Police Cottage, a two-storey, probably Edwardian, building with pebble-dashed front. The tiled roof replaced the original thatch in 1910.

Next door is the tiny thatched, brick and timber cottage, Little Deane, originally the shepherd's cottage, of 17th-century brick, two storeys, timber-framed and thatched. The interior has fine oak beams.

Beyond the little house stands, further back from the lane, Deane Cottage, the Elizabethan farmhouse of Deane Farm. It is a very fine example of the period, with two storeys, timber-framed, partly brick, with thatched roof. It still retains its bread oven and cellar.

Beyond Deane Cottage are some modern houses and cottages; then at the end of the hamlet stands the 18th-century Deane Farmhouse, of two storeys in brick with hipped slate roof. The front doorway has fine Doric columns and open pediment.

Out on the extreme south-eastern boundary of the parish with Hursley stands in a very isolated position Crabwood Farmhouse. It was being built in 1714 when Sir John Evelyn rode over with his host, Sir Philip Meadowes of Lainston, whose property it was. It is of brick with tiled roof and has recently been considerably modernised. From its windows in 1714 one could see shipping in Southampton Water, an unobtainable view at the present day. This shows how bare the countryside would have been, denuded of trees after the destruction of forests to build the wooden ships of the Navy and the Mercantile Marine in the two previous centuries.

Chapter Sixteen

CENSUS OF POPULATION

THE FIRST population census began in 1801 at which time Sparsholt (3,552 acres) and Lainston (120 acres) were combined and showed a total of 268 inhabitants.

There were 62 inhabited houses with 62 families in them and one uninhabited house. The population numbered 135 males and 133 females. Of the population 264 were working in agriculture and three in trades. Only one person was engaged in nothing remunerative at all.

Thereafter the population grew considerably, reaching its peak for the century in 1881 with 434; Lainston numbered only 14 people.

							Sparsholt	Lainston
1801 ..	..	..	..	..	..	..	268	
1811 ..	..	..	..	..	..	..	317	
1821 ..	..	..	..	..	..	..	370	
1831 ..	..	..	..	..	..	..	357	40
1841 ..	..	..	..	..	..	..	375	96*
1851 ..	..	..	..	..	..	..	419	11
1861 ..	..	..	..	..	..	..	395	33
1871 ..	..	..	..	..	..	..	401	14
1881 ..	..	..	..	..	..	..˙	434	15
1891 ..	..	..	..	..	..	..	412	17
1901 ..	..	..	..	..	..	..	350	34
1911 ..	..	..	..	..	..	..	378	43
1921 ..	..	..	..	..	..	..	378	38
1931 ..	..	..	..	..	..	;;	426	43
1941 ..	..	..	..	..	..	..	—	—
1951 ..	..	..	..	..	..	..	653	43
1961 ..	..	..	..	..	..	..	715	—
1966 ..	..	..	..	..	..	..	790	—
							(230 males)	
1974 ..	..	..	..	..	..		652	—

*A lunatic asylum housing up to 80 patients occupied Lainston House and park at this date.

In the first census of 1801 which included Lainston with Sparsholt certain fuller details are given.

At this time Sparsholt had 56 houses inhabited.

In 1821 there were 186 males and 183 females. This included Lainston.

Some later censuses give fuller details. Sparsholt had in 1831—

    69 inhabited houses (Lainston one).
    75 families(Lainston one).
     2 uninhabited houses (Lainston none).
    65 families in agriculture (Lainston none).
     8 families in retail trade (Lainston none).
     2 in other work.

The population of Sparsholt was 196 males, 161 females. Lainston had 17 males and 23 females.

In this year, too, there were a considerable quantity of details not later taken into account.

Sparsholt had 100 males aged 20, six occupiers employing labour, one not employing labour. There were 72 labourers employed in agriculture, 12 in handicrafts, two educated men, four males of age of 20 not in service, three males aged 20 and over in service. There were also 11 female servants. Lainston had 17 males aged 20, six occupiers employing labour, three men employed in crafts and trade, one educated man, four men aged 20 not servants, three men aged 20 who were servants, five female servants.

1881

Sparsholt had 94 inhabited houses, six uninhabited houses. Lainston had four inhabited houses.

The population consisted of 210 males and 224 females at Sparsholt, and Lainston had seven males and eight females.

1891

Sparsholt had 92 inhabited houses and six uninhabited. It had 209 males and 203 females, in 115 families.

Lainston had four inhabited houses. The population consisted of seven males and 10 females.

1901

Out of a total population of 350 (Sparsholt) and 34 (Lainston) there were 103 families in the former and seven in the latter. This was a very cursory census giving no further details.

1911

Out of a total population of 378 for Sparsholt and 43 for Lainston there were 197 males in Sparsholt and 181 females; in Lainston 19 males and 24 females. There is a note under the heading of Institutions or Large Establishments which gives four for Sparsholt with population of four and one for Lainston with population of three. A unique note in this census gives under the heading Persons enumerated in Barns, Caravans, Sheds, Tents, as three males and one female for Sparsholt, and three males for Lainston.

1. Aerial view of Sparsholt village, 1966.

2. (*left*) Tower and west end of St. Stephen's church, Sparsholt.

3. (*below*) The chancel, St. Stephen's church, Sparsholt.

4. (*opposite above*) Appletree Cottage, Deane.

5. (*opposite below*) The cellar of Appletree Cottage, reputed to have been used by smugglers.

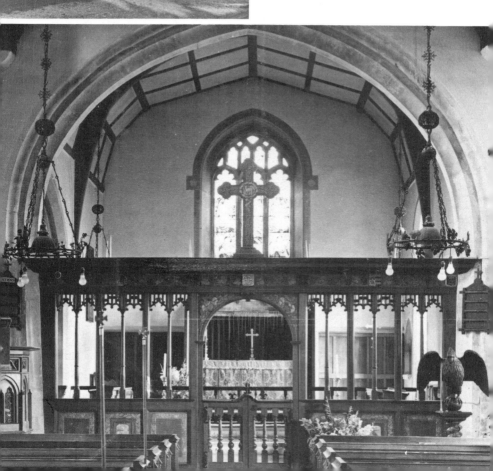

6. The *Woodman* inn, Sparsholt, before conversion to a private dwelling.

7. The *Plough* inn, Sparsholt.

8. Yew Tree Cottage, Sparsholt, which was used as a Dame School during the 19th century. It was demolished in 1974.

9. The Vaine Cottages, Sparsholt.

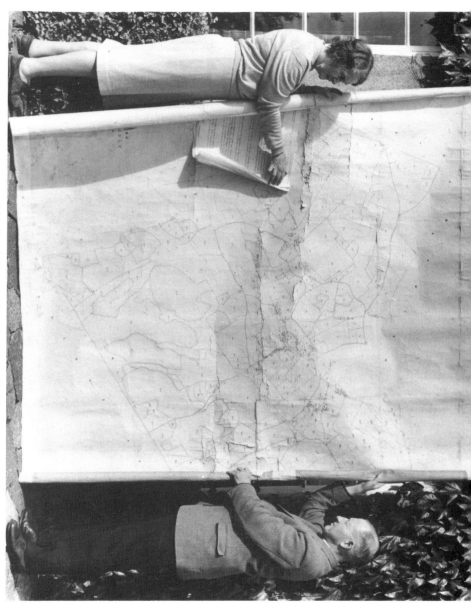

10. The tithe map for Sparsholt, 1846.

1. The mosaic soon after its discovery at the Roman Villa.

2. Room 11 of the Roman Villa, showing the remains of the hypocaust heating.

13. The black pottery bowl discovered inside the hypocaust of a
late-Roman aisled building.

14. The hypocaust where the
black pottery bowl was found.

15. The west front and entrance gate of Lainston House.

16.   The east front of Lainston House from the terraces.

17.   The east front of Lainston House.

18. The lime avenue, Lainston
House, looking east.

19. The 18th-century dovecote,
Lainston House.

20.   The west window of St. Peter's chapel.

21.   The remains of St. Peter's chapel.

Chapter Seventeen

THE ROMAN VILLA

THERE HAS NEVER been a time during which the existence of the Roman Villa in the parish has been completely forgotten. It was used from time immemorial as a quarry for flints needed for road repair and buildings. The south wall of the parish church has undoubted Roman bricks in it and almost certainly the flints there also came from the villa ruins.

In its heyday it was not an isolated property; there had been an Iron Age site slightly to the west, and during the 1972 excavations first century B.C. rubbish pits were found close behind the villa house which had Roman rubbish on top of earlier Iron Age deposits. There had also been Iron Age people in a settlement or farm on Farley Mount under a mile away, 2–300 years before the Romans came, and a 'camp' on a hill to the west on what is now the Forest of Bere Farm.

The villa site occupied a spur running north and south with a clear view in most directions. This spur is composed of chalk with a light capping of flints and was probably scrub-covered in Roman times. Had it been heavily wooded the humus produced by centuries of rotting leaves would have been deeper over the ruins of the buildings.

Iron Age and Roman cultivations in strip lynchets were found on the eastern slope of the spur. This is the truth behind the local tradition that 'the Romans terraced the slope for vines'. That would have been most unlikely in this country on an east-facing slope. In time the uppermost of the lynchets became worn by use into a 'hollow way' leading towards the Roman road from Winchester to Sarum, barely a quarter of a mile away.

The villa was finally destroyed in about A.D. 270–300. Later on the ruins became overgrown and it was partially forgotten, till in 1895 a small party from the Hampshire Field Club and Archaeological Society, led by Messrs. Jacob, Shore and Nisbett, did a day's digging and encountered 'such massive walls and foundations' that they decided it was beyond them to try and excavate further. They did find 'large stone tiles with nail holes' and 'flanged tiles of a hypocaust', also 'tines of stag antlers, ox bones and a sheep or goat horn broken in three pieces as well as a small piece of blue-black pottery'. A more valuable find by a local gamekeeper, Mr. Butler, was a denarius of L. Marcus Julius Philippus (Emperor A.D. 244–9). Unfortunately, none of these finds have survived, though they were apparently sent to the Southampton Museum.

The site was recorded, marked on O.S. maps SU 415 301, but nothing further was done. Only local people occasionally visited the site and, poking around, unearthed a few red tesserae or pieces of tile.

It remained for Edward Bannister, then of Sparsholt, and Robert Carpenter Turner of Winchester to locate the site with accuracy in April 1961. They followed the line of low banks that seemed to demarcate a rough rectangle under the brambles, later measured and found to be 182ft. by 254ft., the extent of the courtyard of the villa. Excited by their discovery they alerted the Hampshire Field Club, whose secretary, Mr. R. L. P. Jowitt, got in touch with the then Ministry of Public Buildings and Works. The Ministry sent down an expert in August 1962, but it took another three years and the threat of an access ride being bulldozed across the site by the Forestry Commission for a full-scale excavation to be mounted. This began in August 1965, directed by Mr. David E. Johnston. It was thanks to the sponsorship of the Department of Environment (late Ministry of Works) that the excavation was begun and brought to such a successful conclusion, and to the Forestry Commission for generosity and help when the actual clearing of the site took place; thereafter through their head forester, Mr. David Percy, showing great interest in the excavation.

The first hour of digging across a narrow ride spanned by a low bank produced some of the 'massive foundations' similar to those of 1895. The 'bank' was actually the debris of the perimeter wall, the foundations of which were just behind it and only about six inches below the surface. A massive corner stone of limestone formed an angle of the wall close by.

Though the whole of the perimeter wall of the courtyard was not opened up in 1965 enough was uncovered to show that it led past the curious long, low mound, 110ft. by 35ft., obviously man-made, that rose 3–4ft. above ground level in the undergrowth outside the line of the perimeter wall. Excavation of the mound began at once and produced the first Roman coin, a denarius in silvered bronze of Claudius Gothicus (*c.* 210–275) with a quantity of painted wall plaster, broken roofing tiles and square red tesserae. Clearly this was the dwelling-house. Excavation was hampered by the necessity of digging through the mound to ground level and then below this; but finally, after removing a great quantity of tiles, tesserae and fragments of painted wall plaster, one digger broke through to the original floor level and revealed a glimpse of a mosaic floor. When the whole of an area 12ft. by 10ft. was uncovered the splendid mosaic was revealed to be in an extraordinarily good state of preservation with only one area of damage where possibly something from the roof had fallen on it when the house collapsed. Partly perhaps owing to the collapse of the whole roof simultaneously (thus covering with the debris and the walls it brought down all the mosaic and tessera-covered floors) do we owe the fine state of the mosaic itself and the wall plaster hypocaust tiles, roof tiles, red and white tesserae and opus signinum floors.

Building 1

Though the dwelling house was ultimately the most important of the buildings in the villa complex, it was not the first Roman building on the site. An earlier rectangular building 30ft. wide and of unknown length, in which the owner, his family, servants and probably animals lived, was built backing on to what became the perimeter wall of the yard and north of the site later occupied by the dwelling house. Though conditions must have been rather squalid he did have a fine three-roomed bath suite on the usual Roman plan—tepid room, calidarium and cold room—which had painted plaster, some of it representing mosaic, a rarity in Britain. The first building was accompanied by an early version of the perimeter wall running west to a corner under the later wall north of the dwelling house.

Contemporary with this first building was probably the well whose collapsed remains now fill a shaft estimated to be over 200ft. in depth. The top has weathered to a huge crater 12ft. deep when excavated. It is a pity that a full excavation of this well was judged to be too expensive to undertake.

The Aisled Building

Perhaps the owner's family increased; it certainly grew older, requiring more room, so the original building was demolished and what has been called 'The Aisled Building' took its place.

This was considerably larger than Building 1. It was also more elaborate. The building was probably intended for the farmworkers who lived there alongside their animals and farm implements, as indicated by the discovery of an iron plough coulter in the debris.

The walls were of flint with limestone bonding courses. The roof, doubtless thatched, was carried on wooden posts, some of whose stone bases have survived. The centre was probably lit by 'clerestory lighting'.

Lack of privacy with no interior wall encouraged the building of partitions between the pillars and the outer wall, dividing the communal residence into a series of rooms. Two of these, Nos. 12 and 13, were later given mosaic floors and in one of them in 1972 the pedestal of the statue of possibly the house god was found. The figure had not survived.

The simple bath suite contemporary with Building 1 was replaced by a more elaborate suite complete with warm room and apodyterium. One would enter either the plunge bath with steps and tiled bottom, or the caldarium, a hot room with red opus signinum (cube-shaped tesserae) floor and hypocaust heating. The wreckage showed that this room had been vaulted; each apse had a half-dome of light tufa blocks and the double vault was of rubble masonry with ribs of hollow terracotta voussoirs carrying the heat over the ceiling. The vaults were plastered and painted yellow, white and red. Iron brackets on the north wall may have fastened a wall surface such as a precious marble veneer.

The Main House

Lack of privacy eventually drove the owner to build a house 110ft. by 35ft. at a little distance, facing the perimeter wall and at right-angles to the Aisled Building. This would face across the walled yard to the entrance gates. It would have been one storey high, roofed with grey limestone slates except for the rooms at each end, which had red tiles. Windows were mostly unglazed; the only stratified window glass found was in Room 11. All the rooms were decorated with painted plaster in green, yellow, white, red, and pale plum colours. Reconstruction of some of this has produced a fine portrait in a roundel of presumably the lady of the house.

The entrance was in the centre of the verandah which looked on to the courtyard. This verandah had a red and grey tessera floor in a double key pattern. Immediately behind this was the main reception room (7) whose geometric mosaic floor was the showpiece of the villa. It shows an eight-pointed star in a circular border of wave pattern, double key pattern and single guilloche, the whole set in a panel of quadruple guilloche. Two spandrels contained a simple fan with bright blue centre; in the other two was an interesting hybrid motif—a half open bud of a conventional type with tendrils, but with the lower half unmistakably that of a cup, having a band of jewels across it and a solid triangular foot.

Thanks to a most generous response to the public appeal organised by the Hampshire Field Club and Archaeological Society, and a donation from the then Ministry of Works, the mosaic was lifted in May 1969 and is now displayed in the Winchester City Museum.

The date of the mosaic is indicated by a *mortarium* sherd used as a tessera in the floor of Room 6, its contemporary, which belongs to the late third or early fourth century.

Room 2 with its red and grey checkerwork floor and a burnt patch where perhaps a brazier stood, is at the quiet end of the house next to the chalk-floored Room 3—perhaps a bedroom and study.

Room 4, at 19ft. by 18ft., the largest in the house, and Room 8 beyond the Mosaic Room (7) had red tesselated floors. Finds suggested that 4 was a living room with a brick stove set in the south wall, while 8 with red and saffron walls was warmed by the next room (11), another living room, with hypocaust heating. No. 9 had a red and grey floor, and No. 11 a mosaic floor, mostly lost. Room 10 led into the verandah, and had a chalk floor with hearth and bare walls. Could this have been the kitchen?

Room 5 seems to have been a store room with chalk floor, but one corner concealed a pit covered with slabs and containing the body of an infant—possibly a dedication?

Room 6 had a tesselated floor—perhaps a guest room?

Room 9a had no wall plaster and a most uneven floor. It contained the fuel store and stokehole for the hypocaust under Room 11. Oddly this smoky place was entered from Room 9, a smart little ante-room which was entered from the verandah and had a red-tesselated floor. It cannot have been part of a bath suite as it was not connected to Nos. 8 or 11. The latter was heated by a solidly-built channelled hypocaust whose box flues survived in the walls. Part of the mosaic over the floor heating had survived *in situ*.

Two coins from the rubble of the house were of Claudius (210–275) clearly a survival, and Allectus (293–296). The latter murdered his commander-in-chief, Carausius, in A.D. 293 and assumed command of the breakaway British province and fleet. In 296 he was defeated in a land and sea battle by Constantius and lost his life in or after a battle somewhere to the north of the villa, probably near Silchester.

The coin was minted in London and the denomination, a quinarius, is uncommon.

The Barn

This was a single-storeyed building situated outside the courtyard, the perimeter wall of which formed its northern wall with entrance into the central and western rooms (21 and 22a), probably into Room 20 as well. The long central room had a cart-sized entrance, later blocked. It measured 55ft. by 18ft., with an earth floor and flint walls rendered with mortar. As there was no sign of animal occupation it was probably used as a barn. The western room (22) had been re-floored with discarded stone roof slates sealing a coin of Tetricus (270–274) and a useful group of pottery.

The Main Entrance

A complex of intersecting pits in the centre of the perimeter east wall facing the main house. The earliest gateway consisted of two roughly rectangular posts in pits, about 10ft. apart, presumably with a single gate. This was replaced with a monumental gateway in flint set on colossal flint and chalk foundations in pits. The superstructure of this was later demolished to be replaced by a double gate hung on wooden posts with a central stop. Finally the gate was narrowed, one post renewed, and presumably a single gate hung on it.

The Timbered Hall

This last building to be constructed on the now decaying villa property dates to the fourth century. Of completely different character from its predecessors, it rose outside the south corner of the perimeter wall east of the Barn. All the material was plundered from the earlier buildings; pila bricks from the hypocausts, flint and squared stone from the nearest corner of the Barn. There was no foundation trench for the footings of the walls, and yet these supported a massive superstructure, 60ft. by 40ft., presumably timber-framed and with thatched roof. One entrance only was found, with massive tree-trunk posts set in stone-packed pits. Faint steps in the chalk led away from the Hall down to the hollow way—once the approach to the villa.

There must have been two series of wooden pillars to support such a wide-spanned building. The floor was of rough re-used flints, and the lay-out suggests that though occupied by people and their animals a certain segregation was in operation.

Cooking on a well-used kiln or oven went on inside the building. It was partly constructed of pila hypocaust bricks from the Main House or the Aisled Building.

An infant burial was partly disturbed by the building of the south wall of the Timbered Hall. Possibly not dedicatory the child may have been buried long before in open ground outside the perimeter wall well away from the Villa house.

The doorway of the Barn was blocked probably late in the villa's existence. If the perimeter wall were still intact such action and the final single gate phase of the entrance might indicate the sealing of gaps in the perimeter wall, the space within being retained as a stock-yard. Whatever the date of this it is important to note that nothing distinctively post-Roman or early Saxon has been found on the site.

Chronological Summary

Period 1.—Prehistoric. Bronze age arrowhead. Storage pits, possible ditches and pottery of Iron age type. Lynchets.

Period 2.—(a) Early Roman; (b) Building 1 and the Well.

Period 3.—(a) Late second, early third century. Aisled Building; (b) third century. Sub-division of Aisled Building and insertion of Hypocaust Room 15.

Period 4.—(a) Late third century (?). Main House; (b) Hot Room 15 replaced by brick-built bath suite. Rooms 17 and 18. Rooms 12 and 14 formed.

Period 5.—(a) Barn; (b) perimeter wall added probably immediately.

Period 6.—Fourth century. Tesselated and mosaic floors in Main House and Aisled Building. Entrance rebuilt and twin-towered gateway made probably at this time.

Period 7.—Maintenance and repair. Barn re-roofed. Gateway
demolished and replaced by simple double gate.

Period 8.—Dereliction and systematic demolition. Entrance
rebuilt for last time, but other exits blocked. The
walled area probably used as stock-yards. The Timbered
Hall constructed from the debris of destroyed buildings.
The fields probably still cultivated.

The Last Years

The Sparsholt villa seems to illustrate the cliché that the
Dark Ages began during the Roman occupation. This is
borne out by one distinctive pot which to some eyes has a
Romano-Saxon look. It is paralleled at Rockbourne, Port-
chester and Lankhills (Winchester), in one case with a date
of *c.* 330. This near-perfect black double-handed pot was
found in the hypocaust in Room 15 of the Aisled Building
with unequivocal evidence (a few grains of corn in the
bottom) that the hypocaust had finally been used for corn
drying.

At this time the living-rooms in the Aisled Building
(12-14) were used for storage (a plough coulter and a bag
or box of nails were found) while it was partly derelict,
judging by the deterioration of the mosaic floor. The central
rooms were demolished, perhaps for the sake of their
materials. All the walls had fallen outwards, broken off at
their foundations; concrete floors in the bath suite had been
broken up to salvage the pila bricks. All the special ridge
tiles from the Barn were removed.

The Main House, now unoccupied, was left to decay. The
very fact that this happened without deliberate destruction
probably preserved for us the splendid mosaic, the wall
plaster and the tesserae. It seems almost certain that the
collapse of the roof through decay of the timbers brought
down the walls all at one time thus to create that long low
mound of scrub-covered earth that was so intriguing a feature
of the site, lying in the undergrowth outside what proved
to be the perimeter wall of the enclosure.

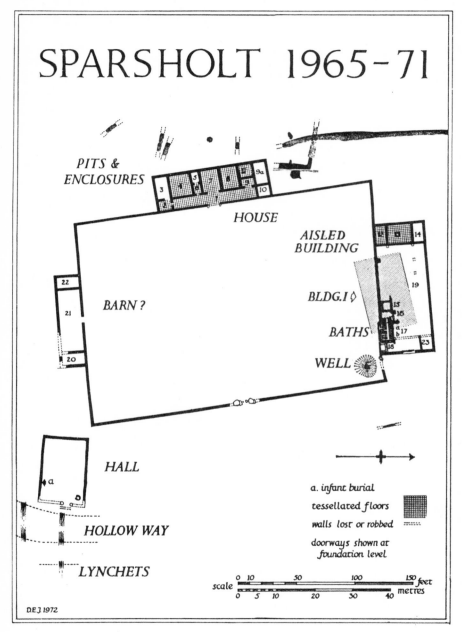

SPARSHOLT 1965-71

PITS &
ENCLOSURES

3

5

9a

10

HOUSE

AISLED
BUILDING

14

BARN ?

22

21

20

BLDG.I

19

15

16

BATHS

17

23

18

WELL

HALL

a

b

a. infant burial

tessellated floors

walls lost or robbed

doorways shown at
foundation level

HOLLOW WAY

LYNCHETS

scale

0   10   50   100   150 feet
0   5   10   20   30   40 metres

DE J 1972

Plan of the Roman Villa, Sparsholt

LAINSTON

Chapter Eighteen

LAINSTON

THE PARISH OF LAINSTON, 2½ miles west of Winchester, consists of 120 acres with a population made up of the inhabitants of Lainston House and the estate. When the last separate census was taken, in 1921, it was thirty-eight.

In shape it is more or less oblong with fairly straight sides on the north and west, but with an irregular indented outline on the south where the boundary seldom follows a road or path and eventually cuts across the famous lime avenue on the east by a line no longer visible and joins the Stockbridge road which forms its northern limit. On the south-east and west it is encircled by the parish of Sparsholt from which it is still ecclesiastically distinct, though the benefices were united in 1928, and it sends its own representative to the Sparsholt Parochial Church Council. For civil purposes it was united with Sparsholt in 1932.

Several variations of spelling occur throughout its history, e.g., Leynestone, Lenistone (13th century), Launston (17th century), Lanistone (17th century).

The Manor of Lainston

At the time Sparsholt was included in the Manor of Chilcomb in the gift of King Cynegils in 633 it is possible that the small manor of Lainston was included in the gift. There were, however, lands held independently of the Prior and Monastery of St. Swithun by Godfrey de Caritate which descended on his death to his son John who was in the service of King John in 1215 and 1216. After the dispute over the advowson of Sparsholt (see chapter on The Church)

125

it is possible that the Manor of Lainston was separated from Sparsholt. In the Selborne Parish Charters (Hampshire Record Society, 1894) there is mention of a certain Simon de Wincestre who held Lainston 1285–1290. There is also mention of it as a separate manor in 1342.

Fromond's Court

Another small manor, Fromond's Court, is now unidentifiable, but may have been part of Sparsholt or Lainston. It took its name from the family who were natives of Sparsholt, one of whom, John Fromond, built a chantry in Sparsholt church before 1420.

The Fromonds were granted a parcel of land in 1258 and this was known as Fromond's Court. It passed to the Skillings who combined it with their Manor of Lainston.

Lainston House and its Owners

It is not known exactly when the original house of Lainston was built, though there are ancient foundations in the cellars which may date from the 11th or 12th centuries.

The present house dates from the late 17th century, built on the remains of an Elizabethan structure of which there are traces in the stone mullion of windows in the basement on the avenue front.

Charles II certainly stayed at Lainston and legend has it that he leased it and altered it to suit his current mistress, Louise de Keroualle, Duchess of Portsmouth.

It is, in the opinion of many people in the district, the loveliest house of its kind in Hampshire. Built of rose-red brick with stone gables and cornices, it faces on its entrance front a forecourt which is embraced by two arcades. The front is broken up into two slightly advancing gables with a recessed wall in which is the shallow pedimented portico. The facings of the windows are in stone, but the quoins on the outside corners of the walls are of brick. Dormer windows break up the steep but well-proportioned roof and the tall chimneys are exactly of the right height to balance the whole.

Unfortunately, a former owner built at the turn of the century, a nursery and kitchen block which, though admittedly a good copy of the main building, nearly spoils the fine proportions of the original 17th-century block which with its broken front almost forms the celebrated Elizabethan E-shape.

The forecourt faces wrought-iron gates of the 18th century which form the entrance and beyond them looks over a crossing of driveways to another fine pair of wrought-iron gates of the same date which lead to the hexagonal walled garden of the same rose-red brick as the house.

The quadruple avenue of lime trees running from the north front of the house for three-quarters of a mile to join the Winchester road was standing in Queen Anne's day. It is supposed to have been planted in 1716. John Evelyn's grandson mentions it in his diary. It may at one time have continued across the Winchester road along Dean Down Drove towards the racecourse at Worthy Down. It has never been used as an approach to the house. The avenue was originally planted with a flanking screen of firs and beech and the removal of these has rather exposed the avenue to wind, but shows up the limes well.

Terraces originally led down from the house to the avenue with a circular pool below them at the head of the avenue. This was filled in many years ago. It may have been difficult to keep filled with water, standing as the house does on a hill 350ft. above sea level.

The north-east front shows the traces of the earlier house with a stone string course and stone mullions of Elizabethan date to the basement windows. The quoins on this front are of brick on the outer angles of the projecting gables and of stone on the inner.

A few yards to the side of the entrance to the forecourt stands one of the most interesting features of Lainston, an octagonal dovecot, or columbarium, which has space for more than eight hundred doves. The present structure is probably 18th century, but no doubt a dovecot, one of the ancient privileges of the lord of the manor, has always stood there.

There is also an old well-house with a 300ft.-deep well in which a donkey used to work a wheel for drawing up water.

The first owner of Lainston was probably Godfrey de Caritate who was living in the reign of Henry II (1154-1189) but the earliest mention of Lainston so far discovered is an entry in the Record of Taxation of the Tenth and Fifteenth in Hampshire in 1334 (Edward III, 1327-1377), which assessment remained the same for nearly 300 years.

> Hundred of Butlesgat
> Sp'shotte, Dene and Layneston.   L XIII. 3.1111d.
> (£13 3s. 4d.)

It seems by this that at a very early date Lainston was for some purpose joined to Sparsholt, though ecclesiastically it was probably always distinct. Neither place is mentioned in Domesday, but as Church property was exempted from William the Conqueror's Survey, and Sparsholt was included in the gift of the Manor of Chilcomb to the old Minster at Winchester by King Cynegils in 633, it is probable that Lainston formed part of the gift (see chapter on The Manor).

Nothing is known of the history of Lainston until 1342 (Edward III, 1327-1377) when Sir Henry de Harnhulle conveyed by fine one carucate in Lainston and the advowson of the church held by Henry de Laverstoke for the term of his life, to John de Winton and Joan, his wife. It probably descended to him from Sir Robert de Harnhulle, who in 1322 had been licensed to have his confessions heard by a Franciscan, William de Corfe.

John de Winton died seised of the place in 1361, leaving his brother his heir, one Richard de Winton. He was clearly financially unstable; it is known that he owed one Hugh Crane £100 in 1377, for he raised £200 on the manors of Soberton and Lainston in 1383. This did not make him solvent, however, and he was imprisoned a few months later and his property valued so that his debts could be paid. He died almost at once. His widow, Agnes, married again immediately, her second husband being Nicholas Brus.

A charter of 1 November 1383 with a warranty of the manors of Soberton and Lainston and the advowson of

Lainston church was granted to Nicholas Brus and Agnes his wife for their lives with remainder to Richard, son of Richard de Winton (or de Wynchestre).

They seem to have conveyed the manor, however, to Thomas Wolvele and John King, chaplain, and it is not known if the second Richard de Winton was cheated of his inheritance.

The Skylling Family

A long gap now occurs and the manor ultimately passed to Michael Skylling, who presented to the living in 1445. He was of an ancient Hampshire family. Their arms are Argent, two chevrons gules; or on a chief of the last three bezants. Crest: Greyhound courant or, collared and lined sable.

Michael Skylling is mentioned in a document of 1455 as being also 'of St. Clement Danes and St. Mary at Strand, London'.

He was succeeded by either his son or grandson, John Skylling, who presented to the living during the episcopacy of Bishop Wayneflete (1447-1486).

Two of the Skyllings, Nicholas of Sparsholt in 1445 and Thomas of Lainston in 1452, were scholars of Winchester College.

William Skylling was patron of the living in 1475, and John Skylling in 1509. It may have been this man or his son who was Sheriff of Wiltshire in 1520. He was certainly a member of the Lainston family.

William Skylling was patron of the living in 1578, and another William in 1598.

The manor remained in the possession of the Skyllings until 1613 when Edward, Richard and Michael Skylling sold it to Anthony Dawley.

The Dawley Family

Thomas Dawley married Mary, daughter of Sir Anthony Berkesly, an old Leicestershire family, and the Dawleys themselves were evidently of some importance in Hampshire as they intermarried with such old county families as the Whiteheads of Titherly, the Worsleys of the Isle of Wight, and the St. Johns of Farley Chamberlayne.

Anthony, second son of Thomas, married Elizabeth, daughter of John James, and lived in Winchester where he died in 1616 and was buried in the cathedral. He had several children, but only two of the sons affect Lainston history.

Walter, the elder, was born in 1593 and was a scholar of Winchester College, matriculated at Oxford in 1610, and became a Fellow of New College. He married Christian, daughter of Sir Henry Whitehead of Titherly. He was probably the first of the line to establish himself at Lainston as he was seised of the Manor of Lainston in 1623, and died 30 September 1632.

Anthony, his younger brother, was also a scholar of Winchester, having been born in 1613. He survived Walter and acted for the latter's widow, Christian, at the presentation of Edward Lane to the rectory of Lainston in 1637. Mr. Lane resigned in 1667. He was also vicar of Sparsholt.

Walter left as his successors, Henry, Walter, who is described as of Ireland, Constance, who married Oliver St. John of Farley Chamberlayne, from whom descended the family of St. John Mildmay, and possibly Francis. (It is difficult to see how Francis could have been the son of Walter, who died in 1632, as the boy is described as being 25 at the time of his marriage in 1660 to Elizabeth, daughter of George Tery of Winchester. He was most probably the son of Anthony Dawley, as must have been Edward, born 1644, and a scholar of Winchester in 1656.)

Henry Dawley, son of Walter who died in 1632, was probably born in 1620–1622. He was apparently 32 when he died in 1654. His youngest child, Francis, was probably posthumously born as he was born 15 February 1653/4, and buried 25 April 1654. His mother is described in the parish register of Sparsholt as Mrs. Anne Dawley, widow. She was the daughter of John Worsley of Gatcombe in the Isle of Wight.

Before coming to live at Lainston in 1650 Henry and Anne Dawley had lived at Hursley in the old Parsonage

House and some of their children were baptised in the church. The family retained possession of the Parsonage House at Hursley until 1719 when they sold it to Sir William Heathcote.

Anne Dawley died 11 August 1682, aged 64, and was buried at Lainston where there is a stone with the arms of Dawley impaling Worsley and the following inscription:

> Here resteth the body of
> Anne wife, widow and
> Mother of Henry Dawley
> of Laniston Esqr.
> And Daughter of John
> Worsley of Gatcombe
> In the Isle of Wight Esqr.
> and who deceased August
> the 11th 1682
> aged 64.

It is interesting to note that while the baptisms of several of Henry and Anne Dawley's children are entered in the Sparsholt register this occurred only during the time that Edward Lane held the rectory of Lainston (1637-1667) while he was also vicar of Sparsholt. During that time he entered the death of one child and the baptism of four others of the Dawley family, though curiously there is no mention of Henry Dawley's own burial which must have been in 1654, so he cannot have been buried there. These Dawley entries seem to show that there can never have been a separate register for Lainston.

When Edward Lane ceased to be rector (1667) for some reason he did not allow his successor, the Rev. James Garth, to make any entries in the Sparsholt book, and the parish went on without any register book at all until the celebrated one made in 1759 by Elizabeth Chudleigh.

The following entries appear in the Sparsholt register:

1650.   Anthony Dawley ye son of Mr. Henry Dawley gent, and Anne His wife was buried at Launston on April 5th

        Cicely ye daughter of Mr. Henry Dawley and Anne his wife was baptised at Launston July 8th.

1651.   John ye son of Mr. Henry Dawley and Anne his wife was baptised at Launston November 18.

> 1652.   Charles ye sonne of Mr. Henry Dawley Esq and Lady
> Anne his wife was baptised at Launston Dec. 16th.
>
> 1653/4. Ffrancis ye son of Mr. Henry Dawley Esq. and Lady
> Anne his wife was borne Feb. 15 and baptised at Laun-
> ston ye 20th of ye same month.
>
> 1654.   Ffrancis Dawley ye son of Mrs. Anne Dawley widow
> was buried at Launston April 25th.

Besides these children there must have been several others:
Walter baptised at Hursley 1645/6, followed by Anthony
baptised there 31 August 1647, and a daughter born 1648,
as well as Anne in 1649. A tombstone in Lainston church
bears the following inscription:

> Here resteth the body of Mrs
> Anne Dawley, second daughter of
> Henry Dawley Esq and Anne
> his wife who deceased the 6th
> day of Decem. Anno Dom. 1679

Henry Dawley, son of Henry and Anne, matriculated at
Wadham College, Oxford, on 28 April 1659, and is said to
have been a Justice of the Peace for Hampshire and to have
been 40 at the time of the Visitation in 1686. He was married
twice, first in September 1670 to Mary Collins, who was 19
and daughter of Anthony Collins of the Middle Temple.
She died on 29 August 1677 and is buried at Lainston. On
her stone is engraved

> Under this stone lyes
> Interred ye body of Mary
> Wife of Henry Dawley
> of Lainston Esqre
> who deceased August
> ye 29 Anno Dom. 1677

Henry married again in May 1693, a widow of 38, one
Anne Hall. He appears to have died in 1703, though even
in the 1880s when Mr. Heathcote made some researches
at Lainston the inscription on his stone was barely legible.
On it is his coat of arms impaling that of his wife.

His widow Anne lived for a good many years after him
and was a cause of a good deal of friction to the incoming
Heathcotes at Hursley Place.

Whether they had any children is uncertain, though an entry of burial of a Mrs. Anne Dawley on 28 October 1758 might refer to a daughter.

Henry Dawley's children by his first wife, Mary Collins, were Anthony (who must have been born before 1677, when his mother died, but is given in the Dawley pedigree as being seven in 1686), Anne, Mary, and Frances. Nothing is known of the latter, but Anne married the Rev. Charles Strangways, rector of Maiden Newton, Dorset, and had one daughter who died at 23, only a year after her marriage. Mary died unmarried in 1715 at Maiden Newton.

Anthony, the only son of Henry and Mary Dawley was High Sheriff of Hampshire in 1707. It is not known if he married and the reference in the Sparsholt register to a Mrs. Dawley living at Lainston in 1708 may refer to his stepmother. This entry records the death in childbirth of a Mary Browne on 4 September 1708, 'A servant to Mrs. Dawley of Lainston'.

Anthony was also Commissioner of Taxes and died in March 1724.

In the first flush of relief at the Restoration, from which date the present house roughly dates, the Dawleys may have over-built themselves and have come to financial disaster.

An extract from the diary of Sir John Evelyn, Bart., of Wotton, Surrey, a grandson of the diarist, gives an account of a visit paid by him and his wife to Sir Philip Meadowes at Lainston. With them went his mother-in-law, Mrs. Boscawen, who was also the mother of Lady Meadowes. Sir Philip had bought Lainston only two or three years earlier.

July 5th 1714

My wife and I with Mrs. Boscawen sett out for Lainston, Sir Philip Meadowes' seat in Hampshire. After passing through Guildford and Farnham the road betwixt these places being on a ridge you have a fine prospect on each hand, we came to Alton, where we waited till past five, the horses being so hot with their mornings work that they would not eat in a long time. We reached Alresford where there is a pond of several acres, about 7. But our own horses being left here Sir Philip Meadowes brought us to Lainston by nine. A little without the town [Alresford] we crossed the river Itchin that runs to

Winchester leaving Abbotstone, a house of ye Duke of Bolton's and the Grange, Mr. Henleys' on the right hand; most part of the way was over fine downs till we came to Littleton, a village a mile on this side of Lainston. Sir Philip, Lady Meadowes and her pretty daughter were ready to receive us in the Avenue, a green ascent of near three-quarters of a mile, and conducted us into the house very much improved by alterations and additions of conveniency since I saw it in 1710 before they bought it of Mr. Dawley.

July 6th

This morning we spent in viewing the house and gardens; from the hall door and all the windows of the east, Mr. Evelyn's house about 4 miles distant, lately built, Mr. Bridges about five miles off, Alresford town about nine, an opening between two woods near Alton about sixteen, and another foresight in ye way to Petersfield, which together with the intermediate down, cornfields and woods, form a very pleasant Landschip.

The garden which is small lies to ye north and from that you see Crawley, a village about 4 miles off and a fine country about it. The south front is the longer being by the addition of some rooms near a hundred foot. The view from it is bounded by some rising ground about a mile off. A little way from the west front is a building scarce finished, half of which is designed for a stable and the rest for a waterhouse and offices, with servants rooms over them. Adjoining to the South is a little Chapel of ease in which there is preaching once a month. At other times they go to Sparsholt, a church in a village hard by. In the afternoon Sir Philip carried me to his sheepwalk called Bushey encompassed with woods, and from thence to Becon Hill, a view of the sea about ten miles off and the Isle of Wight. In our way home we called at a new farm of his situated in a place called Crabwood much higher than Lainston, from one of the windows may be seen plainly the arm of the sea that comes up to Southampton and vessels upon it.

July 7th

I took a tour with Sir Philip to the North of his house by Littleton, Crawley Common, a fine turf on the side of which runs a quickset hedge planted by Sir Philip to fence his ground and so home by Bald down, belonging to him, where he has built a barn and made a pond that has held water this extreme dry season; hither his horses come to drink, there being no water at the house, but what is drawn up by asses out of a deep well.

Though Sir John mentions that his party were met in the 'Avenue, a green ascent of nearly three-quarters of a mile', it is not clear whether the famous lime trees were already planted. They are supposed to date from 1716. The fact that the distance to the house was nearly three-quarters of a mile points to the meeting place being at the top of the avenue where it joined the turnpike from Winchester to Stockbridge. The Evelyn party who came clearly along the Itchen valley, thus avoiding Winchester with its steep hills for the horses, could have come via Kingsworthy and Headbourne Worthy to Littleton and along Dean Down Drove to the top of the Avenue.

Before the Merrills bought Lainston, the first Sir William Heathcote of Hursley was thinking of buying it in spite of having plans to build Hursley Park which he later did build. Mrs. Anne Dawley, stepmother of Anthony Dawley and widow of Henry Dawley who died in 1703, was at that time living at the parsonage at Hursley and seems to have been a thorn in the flesh of Sir William. In his letters he describes her as 'a notorious litigious woman', 'a very tall woman not above 62 years of age and old women are often very tough', and 'Wished the cold tea she drank on her journey may have put her into a good humour when she came to Winchester'.

Finally he got his way and obtained possession of the parsonage, and presumably the patronage of the living as well, which was probably his aim. In any case he had to pay Sir Thomas Trollope £3,420 for the reversion and £71 5s. 0d. interest on the purchase money for five months as well as £2,000 to Mrs. Dawley for possession of the parsonage itself.

John Merrill, who bought Lainston from the Dawleys or Sir Philip Meadowes, started off his occupation by a kindly act of generosity to Sparsholt church. In 1721 he and a certain Mr. Hobbs Weeks presented and erected at the west end of the church against the tower the oak gallery referred to in the chapter on the church.

Nothing is known of the history of the Merrills before they came to Lainston. They may have been a branch of the Wiltshire family, some of whose members emigrated to America from Salisbury in 1634–5.

John Merrill was M.P. for St. Albans and married Susannah, second daughter of Hugh Chudleigh and his wife Susannah, a daughter of Sir Richard Strode. Both the Chudleighs were buried in St. Martin's, Westminster, but were removed to Lainston church in 1721–2, as the following inscription on the tombstone, still fairly legible, shows:

> Here lies interred the Body of Susanna Chudleigh the daughter of Sr. Richard Strode of Newinham in the County of Devon by his wife Anne Drake the daughter of Sir John Drake of Ash in the same county, Bart. She was marryed to Hugh Chudleigh Esq, son of Sir George Chudleigh of Ashton in the said county of Devon, Bart. by whom she had three sons and four daughters and dyed the 27 of January 1716 in the 61st year of her age. Also near this place is buryed Mr. Chudleigh her husband who dyed the 20th October 1707 in the 63rd year of his age. Removed here from St., Martin's Westminster upon rebuilding that church, deposited here Jan 23 1721/3.

Mrs. Susannah Merrill, who died in 1742, was buried at Lainston, and her burial was the first entry in the celebrated register which Elizabeth Chudleigh (Hervey) induced Mr. Thomas Amis, rector of Lainston to make in 1759.

The entry was:

> The 22nd August 1742 buried Mrs. Susannah Merrill relict of John Merrill Esq.

John and Susannah Merrill had one son, named after his father, who succeeded to Lainston on the death of John Merrill, senior, in 1734. He was made a Fellow of the Royal Society in March 1744/5. He married on 14 July 1737 'Mrs. Mary West, otherwise Killigrew' at Lainston 'chapel' and the marriage was registered in the cathedral register, the marriage licence having given permission for it to take place either at Lainston, Sparsholt, St. Bartholomew's, Winchester, or the cathedral.

'Mary West's, or Killigrew's grandmother, Frances, daughter of Sir Peter Killigrew, married Richard Erisey, Esq., of Erisey, and their daughter, Mary, married Colonel John West of Bruton, Co. Somerset. Mary, elder daughter and co-heir of Colonel West, having taken the name of Killigrew, married John Merrill.' (Lysons' *Britannia. Cornwall*, p. 102 note.)

John Merrill, the second, died at Lainston and was buried there on 7 February 1767.

The sole issue of his marriage was one daughter, Mary, who married the Rev. Robert Bathurst, rector of Dennington, Essex, at St. George's, Hanover Square, on 16 June 1759. He died in 1786, aged fifty-eight. They had two sons, Peter Merrill and Robert. Peter Merrill Bathurst seems to have died in the same year as his father, though Tunnicliff's *Survey of the Western Circuit* states that he was the owner of Lainston in 1791. Robert, however, the second son, died in 1791, both died without issue, and the estate came to General Henry Bathurst, son of Peter Bathurst, Esq., of Clarendon Park. The family do not seem to have lived at Lainston since the time of the Rev. Robert Bathurst.

The Bathursts

The General also died without issue, and he left Lainston to the descendants of his eldest sister, Selina, who had married first, Arthur, Lord Ranelagh, and secondly, Sir John Elwell. Their daughter, Selina Mary, married Felton Lionel Hervey, grandson of John, 1st Earl of Bristol, by his second wife Elizabeth Felton.

Selina and Felton Hervey had among other children, Felton Elwell Hervey, who took the name of Bathurst in addition to Hervey in order to succeed to Clarendon Park. He was created baronet in December 1818. He was at one time A.D.C. to the Duke of Wellington. He died without issue and was succeeded by his brother, Frederick. Anne Hervey also subjoined the name of Bathurst. This second baronet married Jane Douglas, daughter of Joseph Hutchinson and had among other children Frederick Hutchinson, who succeeded him in 1824. This Sir Frederick, 3rd baronet, married Louisa Mary, daughter of Walter Smythe, Esq., and had among other children Frederick Arthur Thomas, born 1833. He succeeded his father as 4th baronet in 1881, and in 1897 sold Lainston. The Hervey Bathursts had for a long time leased it to various tenants as their family seat had been Clarendon Park, Wiltshire.

From 1798 to 1805 one Andrew Boyne was tenant and may have sub-let it to George William Ricketts, who had married Laetitia, third daughter of Carew Mildmay, Esq. Their son, Henry, was born at Lainston in 1802.

Nothing more is known about the house till 1821 when a Mr. Powlett, a relation of Lord Baysing, was presumably tenant, as he died there in March 1821.

For another four or five years Lainston remained empty and from 1825–1846 was leased to a Mr. Twynham who ran it as a private lunatic asylum which at one time held more than eighty inmates. It was after the end of this tenancy that the theft of the lead from the church roof took place.

In 1859 a certain John Tregonwell was tenant to the Hervey–Bathursts, but evidently let the farm which was worked by one Henry Watkins of Winchester.

In 1878 Mr. James Scott Barnes took a lease of the estate, but died suddenly at a Vestry meeting in Sparsholt on 28 March 1895. It was a niece of his, Miss Everett, who kept house for him, who also took on the education of all such children of Sparsholt and Lainston, whose parents could not afford to pay the twopence a week per child that was the charge made for schooling in the original Dame's school in Sparsholt.

Mr. Samuel Bostock was the buyer when Lainston was sold in 1897 and he sold it in 1921 to Mr. John Craig Harvey. He died in 1960 and the present owner is his eldest son, Mr. Andrew Craig Harvey.

The Church of St. Peter

This tiny building measuring barely 40ft. by 27ft. is usually mentioned in its early history as a chapel. It dates probably from the 12th century, during which time also the original house was almost certainly built.

Though the church is a parish church it was mostly used as a private chapel of the owners of Lainston at which their tenants and employees attended service.

There are traces of 13th-century work in the windows, but as the building now consists of the three walls only, the eastern one being entirely demolished, it is difficult with any accuracy to say much about its construction.

Amongst the Sparsholt records there is an account to the churchwardens for 'works done in the church belonging to Lainston' during the year 1813 by William Good.

	£	s.	d.
5 days bricklaying and labour	1	10	0
To hair		2	6
	1	12	6
To 3 sacks of lime		8	0
To one hundred of plain tyles..		5	0
To Caridge and Gravel		10	0
	£2	15	6

A note in another very minute handwriting below states that 'Mr. Arney told the churchwarden he would not pay Lainston part. £2.15.6.'.

However, the whole bill, which included certain items for Sparsholt church as well, seems to have been settled to Good's satisfaction on 2 July. This looks as if some attempt had been made to repair the church at this time.

According, however, to an undated letter to the vicar of Sparsholt from the Rev. William Tugwell, who was rector of Lainston 1825–1850, when he died, the church 'fell down' in 1820–1. This was not strictly accurate, though possibly it was already in a very ruinous condition.

From 1825 to 1846 the house was let to the owner of a private lunatic asylum. It was after this tenancy ended that a rascally contractor employed, but not supervised, to carry out removal of the huts in the park in which some of the mental patients had been housed, noticed that the roof of the church contained a rich harvest of ancient lead. No one in authority being there he stripped the lead from the church, leaving the building exposed to the weather. As the Hervey Bathurst agent seldom came to inspect the estate the theft was not discovered till some eight months later, but the family do not seem to have taken sufficient interest in the preservation of. their church to have done anything about it, or to have paid for a new roof though the bad condition of the house after the tenancy of the lunatic asylum was the subject of a law suit.

When in 1850 the Rev. Edward Stewart, who had already been vicar of Sparsholt for eight years, succeeded Mr. Tugwell as rector of Lainston, he obtained permission on 12 December 1850 to discontinue holding services in the church owing to its ruinous condition. In any case most of the inhabitants had been in the habit of attending divine service at Sparsholt for many years, in which church they were also baptised and married and buried in the churchyard. Lainston also had had for a long time a faculty pew in the south aisle of Sparsholt church which was given up after the alterations to that church in 1883.

Successive vicars of Sparsholt, who after Mr. Stewart's incumbency all became rectors of Lainston, occasionally held services in the little church of St. Peter in the summer. This practice has now been revived, and evensong is sung there on the Sunday nearest to the day of the dedicatory saint, St. Peter, when the weather permits.

Chapter Nineteen

THE RECTORS OF LAINSTON

LAINSTON has always been a rectory with the great tithe, such as it was from such a small parish, the property of the rector.

The first incumbent of whom there is any record is John Parson, who may simply have been 'John, the Parson', and is mentioned in 1297 (Pat. Roll, 24 Ed. I Pt. Im.g.).

William Lad was instituted on 15 July 1316 at Lambeth to the church at Laynston, the see of Winchester being then vacant, being presented by Phillip Aubyn, citizen of Winchester, the patron for that turn (Archbishop Reynold's register, f. 57).

In 1333–45, according to William of Wykeham's private notebook in Winchester College Library, Lainston was paying a 'pension' or quota of 6s. 7d. per annum to St. Swithun's Monastery of Winchester. Sparsholt paid a pension too, but a very much smaller sum, 2s., annually.

William Hore resigned the living in 1367 and Thomas Britche, or Brit, was instituted in his place upon the presentation of Richard de Wynchester. In 1379 'Thomas, Rector of the church at Laneston' occurs among the names of the ecclesiastical persons of the Deanery of Winchester who were liable for payment for the Voluntary Subsidy granted to Richard II.

Thomas afterwards exchanged with Henry Goudman, or Gardman, vicar of Aldesworth (Aldworth) in October 1382, the patrons then being Nicholas Bruys and Agnes his wife, of Lainstone.

After him comes a gap which many Hampshire parishes have in the records of their incumbents, it being the time of the episcopacy of Cardinal Beaufort (1404–1447). Of his register, Part I is very sketchy, and Part II has disappeared.

Henry Coleman died in 1445, and John Fleche, or Leche, was appointed on the presentation of Michael Skyllinge.

John Skyllinge was presented to the living by William Skyllinge in 1475.

Philip Walshe died in 1509, and James Fisher was presented by John Skyllinge, senior.

John Casewell was rector in 1520 (Archdeacon's Visitation 1520).

Nicholas Hooker was instituted in 1523 on presentation of John Skyllinge. Hooker was a Wykehamist and Fellow of New College, Oxford, and was only 23 when he came to Lainston. He resigned four years later in December 1527 when he was elected Fellow of Winchester College. He was evidently in high favour with Bishop Fox, then Bishop of Winchester (1501–1529) as the same year he was granted the living of St. Michael's in Kingsgate Street, Winchester. In 1531 Bishop Stephen Gardiner, who had succeeded Fox after Cardinal Wolsey's brief year's episcopacy, transferred Hooker to the joint parishes of St. Maurice with St. Pancras and St. Mary in Tanner Street. Three years later the benefice of Twyford was added to his Winchester livings, and he continued to hold all of them till his death early in 1546 (Baigent, *History of Wyke*).

Robert Dale followed Nicholas Hooker in 1528, but by 1532 services were being said by a Carmelite friar from Winchester. In 1535 Dale was still rector at the time of the celebrated *Valor Ecclesiasticus* of Henry VIII (1509–1547) which was undertaken when the king already had an eye on the wealth of the monasteries. Churches other than monastic came under the survey and at this time the first fruits paid by an incoming priest at Lainston came to 53s. 4d.

Robert Barbour followed Robert Dale on his death and was instituted on 29 August 1541, presented by Charles Bulkely and his wife, Alice.

Barbour resigned in 1543, and Thomas Walshe or Welsh was instituted on 30 March of that year, also presented to the living by the Bulkelys. He compounded for first fruits on 30 February 1542/3. Small as his parish was he indulged in a curate, one John Bennet. In 1556 the curate was Richard Layburn. It is not known if Thomas Walshe resigned or died, but by 1562 John Shalden had succeeded to the living and held it together with Tidworth and Swarraton. He died before December 1573.

William Toste, or Tofte, probably followed him in 1573, but it is known that he was one of many clergy deprived of their livings under Elizabeth I (1558–1603), actually being turned out before 26 May 1578 as that was the date on which **William Taylor** was presented to the living by William Skylling. He died in 1598, and **Peter Roberts** was presented to the living by W. Skeeling, armiger, on 22 June 1598. This Skeeling is almost certainly the same as William Skylling who presented William Taylor.

Peter, or Peirce Roberts (he is called by the latter Christian name in the Sparsholt register book) was buried there on 24 September 1637. Four of his children were baptised in Sparsholt:

Peirce	..	..	..	15 November 1610
John	..	..	..	17 August 1613
Daniel	..	..	..	19 March 1615/6
Martha	..	..	..	21 September 1617

His widow, Dorothy, was also buried at Sparsholt, 1 June 1638.

Edward Lane was presented to the living by Christian Dawley through her brother-in-law, Anthony Dawley; Walter Dawley, Christian's husband and the patron of the living had died in 1635, leaving his children minors. This presentation is also noted as having been made by the Bishop of Winchester (Walter Combe, 1631–1645).

Edward Lane had also been appointed vicar of Sparsholt in 1635, the first incumbent to hold both livings, and he made the following note in the burial register of Sparsholt which he had started, transcribing earlier entries from older volumes or sheets of paper.

A Register of ye names of all such as have been Buryed in Sparsholt since Mr. Airey came to be Vicar here and of all such as have been Buryed in Launston since Mr. Lane came to be Rector there.

This seems to indicate that till Mr. Lane became rector no one had kept a register of births, deaths or marriages at Lainston.

As long as he remained rector of Lainston he continued the practice of entering Lainston events in the Sparsholt register book, but in 1667, when he was made rector of Nursling, he resigned Lainston and the entries for Lainston in the Sparsholt book ceased.

Edward Lane was a writer of note in his day. (See chapter on the Vicars of Sparsholt.)

James Garth followed Edward Lane in 1667, being presented to the living by Henry Dawley on 24 March 1667/8. He resigned in 1671.

John Turner was presented by Henry Dawley on 18 March 1671/2.

Walter Garret was presented by Anthony Dawley on 13 December 1707.

Then comes a gap of some thirty years in the list of rectors and this coincides with the purchase of Lainston by the Merrills from the Dawleys.

Thomas Amis was presented by Susannah Merrill, widow, in February 1737. He was the priest who performed the secret marriage of Elizabeth Chudleigh and Augustus Hervey in August 1744. He was a minor canon of the cathedral, 1736–59, and rector of St. Michael's and St. Swithun's, Winchester. He died in 1759.

Stephen Kinchin was presented to the living by John Merrill on 29 September 1759. As successor to Mr. Amis he was called as a witness in the bigamy trial of the Duchess of Kingston (Elizabeth Hervey, née Chudleigh) in 1776.

Samuel Gauntlett was presented on 17 April 1778 by Robert Bathurst, himself a priest, who had inherited Lainston. Mr. Gauntlett was the son of John Gauntlett, gentleman, of the parish of St. Thomas, Winchester. Samuel was baptised on 3 March 1744/5, entered Trinity College, Oxford, 31 March 1762, took his B.A. in 1767 and M.A. in 1771. He was elected Fellow of New College in 1763 and stayed there till 1777 when he became a Fellow of Winchester College. He studied Divinity, in which he took his B.D. in 1794 and became D.D. the same year. He became Warden of New College in 1794 and died in 1822.

He was also vicar of Hursley with Otterbourne in 1780 till 1804, when he resigned on becoming vicar of Portsea.

Henry Gauntlett was presented on 17 March 1807 by Sir Felton Hervey Bathurst, heir to Robert Bathurst. He may have been a son of Peter Gauntlett of St. Thomas's, Winchester. If so he was baptised on 6 June 1781, went to Trinity College, Oxford, in 1700, and took his B.A. in 1802, and M.A. in 1806. Lainston may have been his first living. He resigned it in 1819.

James Scott was presented by Sir Felton Hervey Bathurst on 5 August 1819, remaining rector till his death in 1826. He was the son of the Rev. James Scott of Southampton and went to New College, Oxford, in April 1794, aged seventeen. He obtained his B.C.L. in 1803, becoming rector of Weston-super-Mare, 1811, and of Lainston eight years later. It was during his incumbency that the little church of St. Peter became completely ruinous, though it still had a roof. How much of the neglect of the building was his fault and how much that of the absentee landlords, the Hervey–Bathursts, it is impossible to be sure. According to his curate who succeeded him at Lainston he was insolvent when he died in 1826.

William Tugwell Williams was presented to the living on 29 April 1826 by a new patron, who may have been a tenant of Lainston, the Rt. Hon. W. H. Freemantle. Mr. Williams was the son of the Rev. Joseph Williams of Avening, Gloucestershire. He went up to Corpus Christi College, Oxford, in January 1799, aged 18, and took his B.A. in 1803, and M.A. three years later. He was Fellow of his College till 1812. That year he became chaplain to St. Cross Hospital, Winchester, and curate to Henry Gauntlett at Lainston at a salary of twelve guineas per year, his duty being to take the monthly service there. He succeeded to the living in 1826 after the death of James Scott, Henry Gauntlett's successor, remaining there till his death in 1850. While he was at Lainston as rector his stipend was £14 10s. 0d. per annum, paid in October by a certain John Hayward of Browfoot, near

Devizes, who was presumably the Bathursts' agent and the careless one who should have noticed the theft of the lead from the church roof in 1846.

Edward Stewart became rector on the death of Mr. Williams in 1850, eight years after becoming vicar of Sparsholt. On 12 December 1850 he was dispensed from holding services at Lainston 'in consequence of there being no church'.

Details of his life are given in the chapter on the Vicars of Sparsholt. He died in 1875.

The rectorial value of Lainston during Mr. Stewart's time was £34, £27 of which came from the rent of land at Liss (see below).

Edward Dawsonne Heathcote succeeded Mr. Stewart in 1875 and was admitted at the same time to the living of Sparsholt. Details of the life of this most beloved vicar and rector are to be found in the chapter on the Vicars of Sparsholt.

It was during his time that the controversy with the Governors of Queen Anne's Bounty over the sale of 24 acres of land belonging to the living of Lainston at Hawkley, Liss, was carried on with considerable verve on the part of Mr. Heathcote and equal obstinacy on the part of the Governors. The origin of the possession of this land is obscure. It appears to have been annexed to the living of Lainston in 1814. In 1875 a certain Mr. James Maberly of Hawkley Hurst, whose land adjoined, offered to buy it for £1,300. The Governors refused, standing out for £1,500. The land was farmed and was rented for £27 per year. Its value, therefore, reckoning 20 years purchase at £27 was £540.

Into this discussion entered Mr. Heathcote with his usual energy, but for a time was unsuccessful in persuading the Governors to reduce their requirement. It took Mr. Maberley's refusal to discuss the matter further and withdrawal of his original offer to make them see sense. They seem to have panicked when the sale appeared to be lost, but it took eight years, with endless correspondence on both sides and between Mr. Heathcote and Mr. Maberley, for the matter to be settled to the latter's satisfaction, and it is not very clear whether he in the end paid £1,300 or £1,500. All that is known is that he wrote to Mr. Heathcote in July 1883 that his solicitors had paid 'the money' on 13 July.

From Mr. Heathcote's time onwards, till the benefices were formally united in 1928 both parishes had the same incumbent.

Chapter Twenty

THE HISTORY OF ELIZABETH CHUDLEIGH

THE NAME Elizabeth Chudleigh nowadays rouses few memories in the minds of most people, but during the last half of the 18th century there were few weeks that one or more of the inveterate letter-writers of that period did not have something scandalous to say about her. Few people have had more vicious, slanderous nonsense written about them than this unfortunate and probably unwitting sinner.

Elizabeth was born almost certainly in 1720, the daughter of Colonel Thomas Chudleigh of Asheton, four miles from Chudleigh, near Exeter, who was at that time in command of Chelsea Hospital for Pensioners. She came of a race of Devonshire gentlemen many of whom had been sailors and adventurers in the tradition of that county of courageous men, and in many ways resembled them. It is not known where she was born, though it is unlikely that her mother stayed in London for her birth; no record in any Chelsea register has been found. Mrs. Chudleigh was a first cousin of her husband, being Henrietta, fourth daughter of Hugh Chudleigh of Chalmington, Dorset. He was a brother of Sir George Chudleigh, 3rd baronet, father of Colonel Thomas Chudleigh.

Henrietta's elder sister, Susannah, married John Merrill of Lainston, while another, Anne, later to have a moment of disastrous influence on her niece Elizabeth, married a Colonel William Hanmer. After the death of Susannah Merrill in 1742 Mrs. Hanmer came to keep house at Lainston for her brother-in-law.

Elizabeth spent her early childhood in Chelsea and played in the gardens with Horace Walpole and his brother and the children of other well-known people. This came to an end with the death of Colonel Chudleigh when she was six, and she and her mother found themselves in straitened circumstances.

Mrs. Chudleigh was a woman of considerable courage. She was returning in her coach to Chelsea Hospital after an evening engagement when she was held up and a pistol thrust through the window with the usual demand for money and jewels. Without a second's hesitation she pushed her head out of the opposite window and shouted to the footman to fire. The footpads made off.

So now, faced with the education and upbringing of Elizabeth, Mrs. Chudleigh abandoned the pleasures of London and probably retired at once to Devonshire where the girl received the amount of education then considered necessary for girls, which was very little. At 16 she was of medium height, inclined to be plump, but with a piquant expression, very charming and with a considerable wit.

In Devon she met Pulteney, later Lord Bath, who interested himself in her and was probably responsible for teaching her more than she would have picked up with governesses. He instilled in her economy, rare in those days, and this stood her in good stead later. She was, however, impatient of study and disliked having to concentrate. One of her sayings to an admirer reproaching her for fickleness was, 'I should hate myself if I were in the same mind for two hours together'.

Joshua Reynolds certainly met her when he was in Plymouth at the start of his career, and he painted her portrait.

It may have been this picture coming to the notice of the Court that led to Elizabeth's appointment to Princess Augusta as maid of honour. It must have come as a great relief to Mrs. Chudleigh as the salary as long as the girl remained unmarried was £400 a year.

Dress in the days of George II was gorgeous, such as to make an instant appeal to a girl with extravagant tastes. Heavy brocade gowns of most splendid materials, with the waist drawn down to a point, were worn over enormous hoops, the wide sleeves being adorned with ruffles at the cuffs. Necks and shoulders were adorned with the finest handkerchief lawn and cambric, and these became so extravagant and expensive that a law was passed prohibiting them except in the most unobtrusive style.

Elizabeth was an instantaneous success in London, and among her admirers was the handsome young Duke of Hamilton who fell violently in love.

She seems to have returned his love and they became secretly engaged, but as he was on the point of leaving for the Grand Tour of Europe, it was decided not to make the betrothal public.

However, nothing could remain private from those inveterate gossip-writers of the Court, and the affair was soon well-known.

Perhaps to console herself for the duke's absence, in the summer of 1744 Elizabeth accepted an invitation from her uncle, John Merrill, of Lainston House, to come and stay for the Winchester races.

It will never be known what made her aunt, Mrs. Hanmer, take up the attitude that Elizabeth had no chance of marrying the Duke of Hamilton. Possibly she thought that his family would do everything possible to prevent his marriage with a girl of ordinary, if gentle birth. She did not know that years later he would marry a lovely, impecunious and by no means well-born Irish girl, another Elizabeth, one of the fabulously beautiful Gunning sisters.

Mrs. Hanmer may, as some authorities state, have intercepted the duke's letters to her niece; in any case the girl appears to have failed to receive any communication from him during that time, so when Lieutenant Augustus Hervey of the Royal Navy came over from Portsmouth to join the party at Lainston for the races, Mrs. Hanmer encouraged the young man in what was obviously on his side a case of love at first sight.

He was the second son of John, Lord Hervey, and grandson of the 1st Earl of Bristol. His expectations of succeeding to the earldom were, at that time, remote.

Elizabeth was also attracted to him. Almost certainly it was a question of pique due to Hamilton's apparent neglect of her and to be neglected by a suitor was an experience to which the lovely maid of honour was unused.

The day after the races the young Hervey invited the ladies of the party over to Portsmouth to visit his ship, the *Cornwall,* of Sir John Davers' Squadron, which was lying at Portsmouth preparatory to sailing for the West Indies.

Later that summer he paid a second visit to Lainston where Mrs. Hanmer encouraged his suit and possibly finally convinced Elizabeth that she had no hope of marrying the Duke of Hamilton. It was possibly Mrs. Hanmer who suggested a clandestine marriage.

Lainston lent itself most conveniently to a plan of this sort. The estate was the parish, the church little more than a private chapel, there was no resident priest, the living at that time being held by a parson living in Winchester, and what was even more convenient there was certainly at that time no register for marriages, births and deaths, all the contemporary ones being, as is known from the Sparsholt registers, entered in those of that parish.

On 4 August 1744 a message was sent to the rector, the Rev. Thomas Amis, at his home in Winchester, requesting him to come to Lainston church, alone, at eleven o'clock that night. Mr. Amis who was paid the meagre stipend of £15 per annum may have thought that the fee offered was the sort of sum he could not afford to forego. In any case he came, as requested.

Elizabeth and Augustus went out, ostensibly to walk in the garden. They were followed by Mrs. Hanmer and her maid-servant, Ann. This woman afterwards married Augustus Hervey's servant Cradock. Mr. Merrill and a Mr. Mountenay, who carried a taper to help the priest read the service, joined the others and they all went into the church, which stood, as it does still, just across the courtyard from the house.

Mr. Amis had arrived, the service was celebrated with Mr. Mountenay holding the taper in his hat, and when it was all over Ann was despatched to see that the coast was clear. They then all returned to the house 'without being observed by any of the servants'. This is the actual account of the marriage given at the bigamy trial in 1776.

There was no signing of the register—for the simple reason that there was none to sign—and Mr. Amis was left to make the proper entry in the Sparsholt book, which it is said, he forgot to do. In fact, he could not have done so as he was not the vicar of Sparsholt and could have had no easy access to the register of that parish. In any case it was not thought necessary, or politic, to have the marriage on record.

The newly-married couple remained together for two or three days, then Augustus rejoined his ship, but did not sail for the West Indies till November, and Elizabeth went back to Court.

Though she may not have thought about it at the time of her marriage, Elizabeth must have realised immediately she got back to London that to publish the news of it would involve the loss of her post as maid of honour, and that so necessary £400 a year. She remained, as she was to do for many years, Miss Chudleigh.

The *Cornwall* stayed abroad till August 1746, and Augustus then visited his wife, but the secret was still kept. He went overseas again to the Mediterranean and did not return till January 1747.

Elizabeth was at this time living in Conduit Street where a stormy interview took place between husband and wife. No one knew, but many gossiped, about what happened at this visit of Augustus, but it is a fact that nine months later a son was born to Elizabeth and was christened Henry Augustus on 2 November 1747 at Chelsea. Somehow she had managed to conceal the fact that she was pregnant. Possibly her mistress, Princess Augusta, who was devoted to her, may have conveniently shut her eyes to the fact.

Ann Cradock was at this time in London with Mrs. Hanmer and in her evidence at the trial stated that she had known about the child's birth; in fact, that Elizabeth had told her it was a boy and that he resembled his father. Nothing more is known about this child, only that he was supposed to have died in infancy.

When she recovered her health Elizabeth found herself in that difficult position of a young beautiful woman, who is secretly married, but is obliged to pose to the world as a spinster. She received many offers of marriage, any one of which would have been well worth her acceptance. She was much in demand at the continual round of routs and parties of that gay age, and Horace Walpole described her as a prominent figure at Ranelagh Gardens. Her old suitor, the Duke of Hamilton, the Duke of Ancaster and Lord Howe were only three of the nobility who proposed to her, and it is said that even her mother was amazed at her turning down offer after offer. It is rather hard to believe that Mrs. Chudleigh knew nothing about the marriage or the birth of the child. She herself, in 1750, was appointed by George II housekeeper at Windsor Castle at a salary of £800 per year, rather, one supposes from Horace Walpole's hints, with the object of the pretty maid of honour showing that old royal roué favours.

Before that it is probable that during the summer of 1748 Elizabeth went abroad to Germany and at this time made friends with the Electress of Saxony who remained always her faithful friend.

Peace with France was signed at the Treaty of Aix le Chapelle in 1749 and England burst into a frenzy of celebrations. There was a royal ball in May followed by another at Somerset House to which Elizabeth went dressed as Iphigenia, according to Horace Walpole 'so naked that you would have taken her for Andromeda'. An old print, possibly deliberately libellous, shows her clad from head to heels in a completely transparent garment with a girdle of leaves around her hips. She shocked even the other maids of honour, who were never easily horrified; the Princess Augusta gently rebuked her and draped the young woman with her own shawl.

However, she pleased King George II very much, he was delighted with her costume, and bought for her at one of the booths at the ball, 'a favour for her watch which cost thirty-five guineas'.

At this time she seems to have been carrying on a financially successful flirtation with him, as her perpetual enemy Horace Walpole broadly hints.

In March 1751 Frederick, Prince of Wales, died, and Elizabeth was reappointed maid of honour to his widow, Augusta, the Princess Dowager.

Later that year the Duke of Hamilton married Elizabeth Gunning, but by that time it is probable that Miss Chudleigh was unaffected. She had begun to take an interest in real estate and perhaps remembering Mr. Pulteney's advice she started to acquire small properties which were later to be of profit to her.

In 1752 she joined the fashionable throng at Tunbridge Wells to drink the waters. She does not seem to have had very onerous Court duties and except when commanded to attend her royal mistress was very free. At Tunbridge Wells she met again the Duke of Kingston whose acquaintance she had made when at Windsor Castle with her mother. They soon became very much attached to each other, but by 1753 Elizabeth was more than ever interested in the acquisition of property. This she managed to effect in her own name, though at her trial she vowed that it had been impossible for a long time for her to buy any land in her own name for fear Augustus Hervey would say she had no right to do so, and claim it as her husband.

However this may be, she took an 81-year lease of land in Hill Street from Lord Berkeley where she built a house and later sold it to Hugo Meynell. Later she brought off a similar transaction in Mayfair.

Where she found the money is mysterious. Her salary was then £600 a year, and at that time she did not have the run of the Duke of Kingston's pockets. In 1757, a year after her mother died, she once again bought land, this time in Knightsbridge.

She was famous as a dancer of the minuet, the correct performance of which took a great deal of practice. She was therefore much in demand and perhaps found life rather more exhausting than she could stand, for by 1757 Elizabeth was thirty-seven. She therefore set about building herself a house on her land in Knightsbridge which was later called Kingston House, and was entirely rebuilt by the duke after their marriage in 1769. Elizabeth's object in building it was to have somewhere more or less rural to which she could retire and no doubt be able to receive Kingston without everyone knowing about it.

For three years after she bought the property she occupied herself with the building of the house, and in this she must have had financial assistance from Kingston with whom, by 1762, her relations were open and notorious.

However, her life was not entirely devoted to house building. The first Earl of Bristol had died, and having been pre-deceased by his son, Lord Hervey, Augustus's elder brother was now the 2nd Earl. He was unmarried and in a feeble state of health; Augustus's prospects were, therefore, far more rosy than when he had contracted that disastrous marriage in 1744.

Now 39, and no longer so fascinating nor in the first bloom of youth, Elizabeth decided that it would be as well to have some record of her marriage if she ever had any chance of becoming Countess of Bristol. Accordingly she made her own arrangements and went down to Winchester.

She met her cousin, John Merrill (his father the elder John Merrill who had witnessed her marriage being now dead) at *The Blue Boar* inn in Kingsgate Street, which stood where now is the Choristers' school. This inn was conveniently placed just opposite the house in which lived Mr. Amis, who had married her and Augustus.

Elizabeth sent for Mrs. Amis, the rector being very ill and, in fact, very near death, and told that lady that she wanted a certificate of her marriage with Augustus Hervey.

In Mrs. Amis's own words at the trial long afterwards, 'I invited the lady to cross the street and come into the house where Mr. Amis was in bed. I went up to Mr. Amis and told him her request. Then Mr. Merrill and the lady consulted together whom to send for and they desired me to send for Mr. Spearing, the attorney. I did send for him and during the time the messenger was gone, the lady concealed herself in a closet; she did not care that Mr. Spearing should know that she was there. When Mr. Spearing came Mr. Merrill produced a sheet of stamped paper that he had brought to make the register upon. Mr. Spearing said it would not do;

it must be a book, and that the lady must be at the making of it. Then I went to the closet and told the lady. Then the lady came to Mr. Spearing and Mr. Spearing told the lady a sheet of stamped paper would not do, it must be a book. Then the lady desired Mr. Spearing to go and buy one. Mr. Spearing went and bought one and when brought, the register was made. Then Mr. Amis delivered it to the lady; the lady thanked him and said it might be an hundred thousand pounds in her way. Before Mr. Merrill and the lady left my house the lady sealed up the register and gave it to me and desired I would take care of it until Mr. Amis' death and then deliver it to Mr. Merrill'.

This account sheds some light on the character of Elizabeth. She must have known that the old rector was dying but had no scruples about forcing herself upon him to get what she wanted. Even in thanking him she seems to have thought only of herself, making no apology for forcing herself on him when he was so ill, only observing that it might make her a very rich woman.

The register book was entitled 'Marriages, Births and Burials in the parish of Lainston'. The first entry ran:

> The 22nd August 1742 buried Mrs. Susannah Merrill relict on John Merrill Esq.

The next entry was:

> The 4th August 1744 married the honourable Augustus Hervey Esq, to Miss Elizabeth Chudleigh, daughter of Colonel Thomas Chudleigh, late of Chelsea College, deceased, in the parish church of Lainston, by me, Thomas Amis.

Six weeks later Mr. Amis died and Elizabeth must have congratulated herself on her forethought. The register over which she had taken so much trouble was duly handed over by Mrs. Amis to Mr. Merrill.

The Rev. Stephen Kinchin, who succeeded Mr. Amis, was not told that any register existed for the parish till, in 1764, Mrs. Anne Hanmer died and was buried at Lainston. A few days later Mr. Merrill, who seems to have forgotten that he had the register, asked Mr. Kinchin to register the burial. The new rector replied that he knew of no such book, whereupon Mr. Merrill then produced the book in which Mr. Amis had made the entry, and taking it out of the sealed cover in which it had remained until then, showed Mr. Kinchin the entry of the marriage and told him that it must never be mentioned.

Mr. Kinchin therefore made the third entry. This ran:

> Buried December 10th 1764 Mrs. Anne Hanmer, relict of the late Colonel William Hanmer.

Then he gave the book back to Mr. Merrill.

Three years later, in 1767, John Merrill himself died, and in going through his papers, his son-in-law, the Rev. Robert Bathurst who had married Mr. Merrill's only child in 1759, found the book and handed it over to the rector, Mr. Kinchin. He took it away with him and made the fourth entry:

> Buried the 7th of February, 1767, John Merrill, Esq.

After this he kept the book himself.

By early 1760 Kingston House as it was called—the building that stands on the site today still bears the same name—was ready for guests. It was lavishly equipped, but Elizabeth does not seem to have had very good taste; the effect was too sumptuous. Walpole said that everything was 'loaded with finery' and that the lady seemed to have collected valuable objects from every man she had ever favoured.

A vast party celebrated the housewarming and Elizabeth and Kingston openly entertained together. There were piles of food and even the attics were luxuriously furnished. These rooms, usually occupied by the upper servants, were not used for them in Kingston House, 'as we have no upper servants', remarked Miss Chudleigh.

The Court and all London society seethed with the scandal of the Chudleigh–Kingston liaison. The royal family, however, and particularly her staunch friend and employer, the Princess Dowager, remained firmly her friends.

George III succeeded to the throne in 1760 and life at the Court went on much as before.

In 1763 another great ball took place at Kingston House with fireworks and vast set pieces in Hyde Park. It was yet another of the extravagant entertainments that Elizabeth adored and that her lover did not really enjoy. However, he seems to have been unable to deny her anything.

Later in the year Kingston's attentions were beginning to take another direction, and though there seem to have been no open quarrels something decided Elizabeth to take another trip abroad, ostensibly to drink the waters at Carlsbad. Here she would have been able to visit her friend the Electress Sophia.

In due course she returned to England and resumed her sway at Kingston House. She must have been wildly extravagant, as even with all the duke's wealth behind her she began to get more into debt than even at that time was the usual fashion, and soon she was borrowing right and left. Even more upsetting than debt were the persistent rumours that began to circulate regarding her marriage to Augustus Hervey, and also that he was said to be contemplating suing her for divorce.

Augustus had had a very distinguished naval career and had shown himself brave and a fine naval officer. He was rich with prize-money after several successful coups in the West Indies. He had also fallen in love with a Miss Moysey of Bath.

Elizabeth was beginning to get stout and to show her age. Her rackety life, her debts and other worries were no doubt telling on her and Walpole's cruel observation that 'There is no keeping off age by sticking roses and sweetpeas in one's hair as Miss Chudleigh does still' was probably more or less true. She was now, in 1768, forty-eight.

After taking advice, in November 1768, Elizabeth decided to sue for Jactitation of Marriage. This ancient law was, in legal terms 'A false pretence of being married to another, a wrong for which the party injured could obtain redress of the suit in the Ecclesiastical Court'.

This has now naturally fallen into abeyance as in England the law is clear about whether persons are married or not. But in the 18th century it could be revived.

It is probable that Augustus and Elizabeth were guilty of collusion at this time. He wanted to marry again and she was as sick of the marriage that was no marriage as he. They met and agreed that it might be possible to have the marriage annulled by the Ecclesiastical Court.

She was to institute a suit in the Consistory Court of the Bishop of London for Jactitation of the Marriage, and he on his side undertook to produce no evidence to establish it.

On 18 August Elizabeth 'entered a caveat at Doctor's Commons to hinder any process passing under seal of the Court at the suit of Mr. Hervey against her 'in any matrimonial cause without notice to her procter'.

In the Michaelmas Term she 'instituted a suit of Jactitation of Marriage in the common form'. The answer was a cross libel claiming the rights of marriage.

What the object of Augustus was in thus doing what he had expressly promised not to do, no one knows, but in the end he stated his claim and gave his evidence so badly that it became clear at once that he could not win. His statement said that there had been a secret *courtship* and a *contract* about which only Mrs. Hanmer knew and that the ceremony had been performed in Mr. Merrill's house in the parish of Sparsholt by Mr. Amis, in the presence of Mrs. Hanmer and Mr. Mountenay, all of whom were dead. Ann Cradock was not mentioned and it was implied that the marriage had been kept a secret from anyone but the three mentioned.

Elizabeth's reply was simple. She denied everything. As there were some falsehoods in part of Hervey's evidence she denied all of it. The witnesses produced before the Court spoke only of rumours of a marriage and she proved that she was universally considered as Miss Chudleigh. The witnesses were not cross-examined and, of course, the register that had been so carefully made was not produced, or even mentioned.

She won her case, was declared a spinster, and Augustus Hervey warned not to pester her any more. Nothing now, could hinder her marriage with the Duke of Kingston.

It is possible that she genuinely had a touching faith in the power of the Ecclesiastical Court to annul her marriage, even though she had committed perjury. As she later made clear at her trial in 1776, no one in the five years in which

she was married to Kingston had made the smallest attempt
to accuse her of bigamy, and he himself had taken great
pains to discover from lawyers that they could marry with
impunity.

On 8 March 1769 the marriage of Miss Elizabeth Chudleigh
to Evelyn, Duke of Kingston was celebrated at St. Margaret's,
Westminster. To make quite certain that everyone should
understand that this was her first marriage she wore white
satin with a flurry of Brussels lace, a point that was
remorselessly recorded by Horace Walpole.

Not long before her marriage, meeting Mrs. Amis,
Elizabeth asked her whether she did not consider 'it was
very kind in his Grace to marry an old maid?'

Curiously enough her marriage caused grave offence, even
at Court. It seemed that as the mistress of a duke she could
be tolerated, but not as a wife.

Kingston was fifteen years older than his bride and in
failing health and it is possible that the life they led, almost
constantly on the move, from Thoresby, in Nottinghamshire,
to his other smaller country seats, shortened his life. There
is no evidence, however, that she was not devoted to him;
but she was restless, dominating and now at last possessed of
sufficient money for all her whims.

They were, however, little in London; finished were the
grand parties and entertainments; the five years of her
marriage were passed almost entirely in the country.

Meanwhile, the widowed Mrs. Amis married Thomas
Phillips who had been butler to Kingston before his marriage,
and Elizabeth induced the duke to give him the stewardship
of one of his estates in Nottinghamshire. Thomas Phillips
appears to have been a bad lot and when later he was dismissed
for his overbearing behaviour to the tenants on the estate he
took a house at Bristol where he died four years later.

On 3 September 1773, the Duke of Kingston died at
Bath and his funeral cortège was one of the most colossal
and elaborate of his time. He was buried at Holme Pierre-
point, Nottingham, in the family grave.

Promptly there was let loose a flood of vicious gossip
about Elizabeth and how she had worked on the duke to

alter his will and leave everything to her. He had, in fact, long before disinherited the nephew, who would normally have inherited the money and estate (though not the title, which became extinct), Evelyn Meadows, eldest son of the duke's sister. This young man had behaved very badly in jilting a young and charming lady of good family, stating that his uncle disapproved of the marriage. This was not true, and Kingston, possibly glad of an excuse, cut him out of his will. Elizabeth was to inherit everything in her lifetime, as long as she remained unmarried, then it was to go to Charles Meadows, Evelyn's younger brother.

As soon as possible after the duke's affairs were wound up, Elizabeth left the country which now held no attraction for her with its abundance of her critics and now active enemies.

She went to Rome. There Clement XIV, recently elected Pope, a man of exceptional brain and now at the height of his powers, received her with the utmost cordiality, granting her privileges usually reserved for princes only. He also lodged her in the palace of one of his cardinals.

Elizabeth in return entertained him with her usual lavishness and indeed gave parties to all Roman society. She had always been passionately fond of the sea and sailing, and now a yacht, especially built for her in England, was brought out to Italy and was actually sailed up the Tiber. This event attracted large crowds.

Meanwhile Evelyn Meadows had not been idle in his determination to overset his uncle's will. Through the duke's late valet, the rascally Whitehead, who had left a quantity of letters mostly of falsehood, but with a few grains of truth in them, he got in touch with Mrs. Phillips, late Amis.

Elizabeth found it necessary to pay a hurried and secret visit to England in July 1774, but chose an unfortunate time as she thereby missed letters from her lawyers warning her that she might be arrested for bigamy if she set foot in England. She managed to get out of the country just in time.

She came to England to consult her lawyer, Field, who was confident that the verdict of the Ecclesiastical Court could

not be upset. Probably the question of buying off Ann
Cradock was discussed. There is a good deal of mystery about
this and Ann's evidence at the trial was tricky and misleading.
It is possible that Elizabeth had paid her some sort of pension,
no doubt to keep her quiet and certain that Ann tried to get
more out of her, probably thirty guineas a year. Elizabeth,
very foolishly refused to give her more than twenty guineas,
whereupon Ann promptly got in touch with Evelyn Meadows.
She does not appear to have been a bad woman and would
probably not have blackmailed Elizabeth. She knew, however, that her evidence about the secret marriage could be
very valuable.

Whitehead, in one of his letters, has a story that Elizabeth
had intercepted or found a letter to Ann Cradock in which
mention was made of her having '£300 in the stocks'. Elizabeth, who had promised her £30 a year if she would live in
a village in the North Riding of Yorkshire, was furious,
having believed Ann possessed of nothing. She therefore
refused to pay any pension at all. Ann contended that the
£300 'came from a place that Captain Hervey had obtained
for her husband in the Customs', and implored Elizabeth
at least to allow her £20 a year. This was refused.

Ann then went down to London and got in touch with
one Fozard, an old servant of the duke's, who kept a livery
stable at Hyde Park Corner. He had married Elizabeth's maid
on her marriage with the duke. Fozard advised Ann to write
to Evelyn Meadows. This she did.

Elizabeth meanwhile was back on the Continent, where
the championship of the Electress of Saxony, her faithful
friend, must have cheered her a little as the storm slowly
gathered in England.

In April 1775 Augustus Hervey succeeded his brother as
Earl of Bristol, and one wonders what were the thoughts of
Elizabeth at his succession.

Meanwhile, considering herself quite safe, she remained
in Rome, but in June 1775 she got a severe shock. Her
Lawyer, Field, wrote that a bill of indictment had been
presented, presumably to him as her representative, and
that she must come home. Worse was to come. When she

tried to see her banker in Rome, a Mr. Jenkins, with whom she had deposited large sums of money and securities, he refused to see her. Again and again she tried; to obtain money to pay for the journey back to England was imperative. Finally in despair she informed his servants that she was remaining on his doorstep till he either returned to the house or allowed her to be admitted, and when Jenkins realised her determination he consented to see her, whereupon she produced a pistol and literally held him up until he surrendered her money. Determination and sheer physical bravery had always been two of her strong points. Jenkins had clearly been bribed to delay her return to England till judgement of outlawry could be obtained. Evelyn Meadows was sticking at nothing.

In poor health and racked with nerves she set off undaunted to cross the Alps, an appalling journey that few women attempted in those days, and finally arrived in Calais barely recovered from the hardships of her journey. Here she met Lord Mansfield, one of her few friends, who gave her a clear account of the charge against her.

She went on to London where she must have been cheered by his friendliness and by many of her old admirers rallying to her side, among them the Dukes of Newcastle, Portland and Ancaster, as well as Lord Mountstuart.

Elizabeth now began to study her own case and the relevant law with considerable vigour. Kingston House was said to be full of law books.

Just at this time, to plague her further, appeared Mr. Samuel Foote and his play *A Trip to Calais* which even at that time of licensed slander was considered to be a little too near the bone and was withdrawn after the Lord Chamberlain had refused licence for its performance. The furore, as of course everyone managed to read it, only added to the misery and strain that Elizabeth was suffering at this time. Incidentally, it seems to have ruined Samuel Foote, for whose vicious persecution of Elizabeth there seems no valid reason, and he died in penury in October 1777.

Faced with a charge of bigamy Elizabeth showed remarkable sagacity. Her lawyers seem to have been less clever, unless they were bribed or careless of their client's fate. Evelyn Meadows had had the bill of indictment made out styling her 'Elizabeth Chudleigh', and this had been passed by a Grand Jury at Hicks Hall. Elizabeth promptly refused to be so styled and demanded to stand her trial as Duchess of Kingston.

In this unprecedented situation the House of Lords lost their heads; they were already highly embarrassed with such difficulties as whether she should be called 'Duchess of Kingston' or 'the lady calling herself the Duchess of Kingston' and whether she could be tried at all unless she surrendered as a prisoner. It was decided to accept her petition, and after delays, preparations to 'entertain' the entire peerage and its families—each peer had been allotted seven tickets—and arrangements to seat them all in Westminster Hall, the trial finally opened on 15 April 1776.

The whole royal family was present and everyone who was anyone flocked to the scene. At this time public executions were considered a quite usual entertainment for gentlemen; Walpole described with some details that of the Scottish Lords who were put to death on Tower Hill after the Forty-Five, so to come to watch an unfortunate lady stand her trial for bigamy, one of the punishments for which was burning on the hand, together with forfeiture of all her estates, was a delightful entertainment which would make splendid news for one's correspondence with absent friends.

Elizabeth's demeanour was, as may be expected, perfectly dignified. Clad from head to foot in sombre black, with tiny white frills at her wrists, she was attended by at least three ladies. Descriptions of their numbers vary. An old print shows her declaiming to the Lords, her head covered with a sort of black turban showing no hair at all. Even her enemies were struck by her bearing and the only criticism they could find was that her figure was bad.

The Lords had somehow compromised with the difficulty of her being a prisoner, by arranging for her to be in the custody of Sir Francis Molyneux, Usher of the Black Rod, incidentally a great personal friend of Elizabeth.

A story went the rounds that she asked if her situation was not very disagreeable, alluding to her being every morning according to the usual custom put into the custody of the Deputy Usher, Mr. Quarme, and in the evening delivered up to the Principal Usher of the Black Rod. She replied quite happily, 'that it was certainly rather *uncomfortable,* but though she had *qualms* in the *morning,* she was amply recompensed by Sir Francis at night'.

Though they sat long hours once they got started the peers frequently adjourned for an hour for refreshment, but they never thought of the prisoner and left her where she sat, with the result that by the end of the third day it became obvious that Elizabeth was exhausted and ill. It was agreed to adjourn for a day.

At the beginning of the trial Attorney-General Thurlow described her disgraceful behaviour with the typical sanctimonious eloquence of the 18th century, when to be discovered in sin was far worse than the sin itself. The Jactitation Suit was blamed entirely on Elizabeth whereas it was well-known that Augustus Hervey had been at least as much responsible.

Ann Cradock was a clever witness, never giving herself away even under stiff cross-examination. She resisted attempts by Elizabeth's counsel to catch her into admitting she had been bribed by Evelyn Meadows, but later when cross-examined by Lord Hillsborough admitted being approached by Fozard with a suggestion of assistance. He had put her in touch with Meadows. On the following day she further admitted sending Fozard's letter to the Earl of Bristol (Augustus Hervey) which looks as if she was trying to find the highest bidder.

Caesar Hawkins, who had attended Elizabeth at the birth of her child, was also called, and he damagingly admitted the birth and also that he had been instrumental in negotiating between Elizabeth and Augustus Hervey with regard to the Jactitation suit.

When Lord Barrington was called to give evidence he was in considerable embarrassment as there is no doubt that at some time Elizabeth had confided to him the fact of her marriage. With great dignity she thereupon declared that she relieved him of any scruples that he might have in giving evidence.

She said, 'I do relieve my Lord Barrington from any obligation of honour. I wish and earnestly desire that every witness who shall be examined may deliver their opinions in every point fully whether for me or against me. I came from Rome at the Hazard of my life to surrender myself to this Court. I bow with submissive reverence to every decree, and do not complain that an ecclesiastical sentence has been deemed of no force, although such a sentence has never been controverted during the space of one thousand four hundred and seventy five years'.

Lord Barrington remained loyal to her and declared he 'knew of no fact which will prove the marriage to my own knowledge'.

Mrs. Judith Phillips (late Amis) was then called. She described Elizabeth's visit to Winchester for the making of the register, and said that the lady had borrowed £100 from her aunt, Mrs. Hanmer, before the baby's birth. Mrs. Phillips had visited Elizabeth at Kingston House and after Mr. Amis's death had given the register to Mr. Merrill. She described how she had been fishing with Elizabeth, who had all her life been a keen fisherwoman, and had also visited her at the duke's house in Arlington Street before their marriage.

The register was then produced and the clerk read out the entries, the burial of Mrs. Susannah Merrill, and the marriage of Elizabeth and Augustus, with the signature of Mr. Amis.

Mrs. Phillips was then cross-examined about the dismissal of her second husband, Phillips, by the duke. This she would not admit but became easily flustered into admitting that Evelyn Meadows had paid her expenses from Bristol to London and that she, her husband and Fozard had met Mr. Meadows at the Turf Coffee House, where she was staying for the trial, and also at Fozard's house.

The Rev. Stephen Kinchin, who had succeeded Mr. Amis as rector of Lainston, finally disposed of the myth of Elizabeth's secret visit to tear out the relevant page of the register as he swore that the book had been handed to him on the death of John Merrill, the younger, and had been in his possession ever since.

On the fifth day of the trial Elizabeth addressed the house. She asked why no one had instituted proceedings during the five years she had been the duke's wife. She declared that she had been forced to bring the suit of Jactitation because she had been unable to buy land as investment in her own name while there was the possibility of Augustus Hervey claiming her as his wife.

She reiterated that she had acted in good faith in believing that the decision of the Ecclesiastical Court was genuine and invincible. She denied bringing influence to bear on the duke to leave her everything, and stated that he had been alienated from Evelyn Meadows long before.

That young man 'had cruelly treated an unfortunate lady, virtuous and beautiful, falsely declaring that he broke his engagement to her for fear of displeasing his uncle. He was cruel to his mother and sister and attempted to avoid service in the war'.

She also declared that if she had feared Ann Cradock's evidence would she not have bribed her? If she had genuinely thought herself married to Augustus Hervey would not bribing Ann Cradock have been urgently necessary?

She had sincerely believed herself free to marry the duke who himself had consulted a well-known lawyer, Dr. Collier. This gentleman had assured the duke that the Ecclesiastical Court's decision was final and conclusive. In addition the Archbishop of Canterbury had granted the marriage licence.

When it was suggested that Dr. Collier should be called to give evidence it was found that he was too ill to appear. It is probable that he would not at that stage have seriously affected the decision of the Court.

At last, all evidence available having been called, the Lords were invited to give their verdict. With the sole exception of the Duke of Newcastle, who said that he considered that she had acted in ignorance, the peers voted her guilty.

Elizabeth promptly pleaded benefit of clergy which meant, if granted, that she would escape the barbarous punishment of being burnt in the hand. This, after further argument, was reluctantly granted.

The Lord High Steward in his final speech produced a typically pompous piece of cant warning Elizabeth that 'if she should ever be guilty of a similar offence or any crime amounting to felony, no such claim [of benefit of clergy] could again be allowed and that she would incur a capital punishment'.

Nothing had been gained by the despicable Meadows who had in fact lost enormous sums in expenses, while his 'aunt' retained the duke's entire estate for life, as long as she remained unmarried.

Elizabeth had probably realised what the verdict would be and had accordingly made her plans. Immediately the trial was over she left in Sir James Laroche's carriage for Dover where her own packet awaited her, and sailed at once for France.

Meanwhile she had already sent out invitations to a grand dinner party at Kingston House on the following night, and even went to the trouble of causing her cousin, Miss Belle Chudleigh, to drive openly about the streets in the ducal carriage, trusting to their likeness to each other to make people think she was still in London. She thus managed to defeat again Evelyn Meadows, who had at once instituted proceedings to prevent her leaving the country.

The unfortunate, though fabulously wealthy, woman now settled temporarily in Calais, where she took a house and for a long time afterwards showed her gratitude to the owners by assisting them with money when they were in difficulties.

Augustus, Earl of Bristol, now set about trying to establish his marriage with Elizabeth. Whether he really wanted divorce, or whether he hoped as her genuine husband thereby to be able to claim all Kingston's money, which by law would have been possible, no one will ever know. It is possible that legal experts told him that there was doubt about the validity of the peers' verdict.

Elizabeth was served with a notice in Calais but ignored it. The case came on at the Consistory Court in London in

July 1776, but the judge suspected collusion, the marriage in 1744 having been undeniably proved. He, however, allowed proceedings to begin against Elizabeth, but the whole case fell to the ground with the death of the earl.

A brilliant naval officer, a brave man forced in his early youth into an unusual position from which he was never able to extricate himself, he arouses one's sympathy. Mrs. Hanmer has much to answer for.

For the rest of her life Elizabeth roved about Europe, buying property in Paris, Rome and Russia.

From her first settlement in Calais she went on to Rome from where news had reached her of considerable thefts from her house. Having settled this she came back to Calais and it is known she was in Paris in September 1776.

Hearing that Evelyn Meadows was still indefatigably trying to have his uncle's will set aside she decided that Calais was a little too close to England. She may have feared an attempt on her life. In any case she left for Russia in her own yacht and reached Elsinore in 12 days. From here she proceeded along the Baltic and on to St. Petersburg, where she was received with immense cordiality by the Empress Catherine the Great, who was fond of the English in any case, and she and Elizabeth had certain characteristics in common which no doubt endeared them to each other. A house in St. Petersburg was put at the disposal of the wealthy English duchess, who proceeded to entertain in characteristic fashion, a taste that she had not been able to indulge since the death of the Duke of Kingston.

Wishing to have some place of her own, Elizabeth now proceeded to buy an estate in Esthonia which she re-named Chudleigh, and built a vodka distillery there. Whether this was a commercial proposition or merely to supply herself with the spirit is not known, but her entertainments were, as usual, lavish. She was entertained in return by the Russian nobility in the wildly extravagant style prevailing in which a whole wooden village would be built, peasants installed to give an air of reality, a mock battle staged on an adjacent lake with elaborate fireworks, a vast fair organised with expensive commodities for sale, and colossal quantities of

food and vodka provided. The whole orgy would continue
for two or three days, varied with vast hunting expeditions
in which enormous quantities of game were killed, ending
at last with the burning of the entire village round which
the peasants danced frantically till exhaustion made them
drop to the ground. This was the sort of entertainment
indulged in by Prince Radziwil.

Elizabeth spent a great deal of time with the Imperial
Court and Catherine even arranged for repairs to the ducal
yacht to be carried out in the Russian naval yards at her
own expense, a testimony of her regard that was unpar-
alleled.

In 1780 the duchess visited her old friend the Electress
of Saxony, and perhaps weary of the Russians and the
considerable amount of exploitation she had undergone
by the nobility and their hangers-on, she left for France,
where she had one or two small properties and a house
in Paris.

In Paris she made friends with the Duchess of Oberkirch,
an Alsatian lady, and with the Duchess of Bourbon. Both
of these ladies, according to the former, had the pleasure of
hearing the Duchess of Kingston read aloud to them her
Memoirs. Apparently she allowed the Duchess of Oberkirch
to copy out many passages. Later that lady stated among
other facts that the early love affair that Elizabeth had had
with the Duke of Hamilton had been ruined by jealous
persons passing on scandal to each of the lovers, and that
she had married Augustus Hervey in a fit of pique.

More and more eccentric and ever restless Elizabeth
continued to flit about France, and finally took a vast
property, St. Assise, near Paris, but did not pay for it.

One day she received adverse news about the condition of
a house about which she was negotiating in Montmartre,
and flew into a violent rage, something she had been prone
to do all her life. This caused what may have been a mild
stroke, but she recovered in a few minutes and demanded
a glass of Marsala, which she gulped down, and ordered
another. Her terrified servants dared not cross her, but waited
as she walked about the room saying she would be better in

a few minutes. Then she said she would lie down on a sofa for a little while. This she did and almost immediately died. She was 68, and the date 28 August 1788, 44 years and 24 days after that unlucky night at Lainston.

The sale of her jewels in London at Christmas 1792 realised £7,400, a very large sum for those days.

*   *   *   *   *

From the evidence given at her trial several small points of interest come to light. It is obvious that services were not often performed at Lainston even at the date of the secret marriage when the church was in respectable repair. One of the questions put to Ann Cradock was 'was there service regularly in Lainston Church, or did the family go to any other church?'.

To which she replied, 'They went to service at Sparshot [*sic*] church'.

When the register was produced and shown to Mrs. Phillips she recognised her late husband's handwriting. The book had not been tampered with, but the words 'was married' had been struck through with a black line which she explained by saying 'It is a repetition—there is "marriage" written in the margin, "August the 24th married". The entry then proceeds "the honourable Augustus Hervey Esq" —which being a repetition I suppose they struck that through with a black line'.

The Rev. Stephen Kinchin in his evidence said that he had succeeded Mr. Amis at Lainston and mentioned that Mrs. Hanmer was buried in the vault of the little church there.

The Rev. John Dennis, who had succeded Mr. Amis as rector of St. Michael's, Winchester, which the latter had held in plurality with Lainston, recognised Mr. Amis's writing and said he had known him well.

It was impossible to call Mr. Spearing, by then mayor of Winchester, who had been the lawyer concerned with the making of the register, as he was said to 'be amusing himself somewhere or other beyond sea, God knows where'. Perhaps Mr. Spearing considered it wiser for his reputation as mayor not to be available.

The famous register has disappeared and much fuss over its loss has been made as if any ancient entries of births, deaths and marriages at Lainston had been lost with it. However, study of the Sparsholt registers will show that ever since it became the law to register births, deaths and marriages, those at Lainston had been recorded in them.

It is clear that, interesting as it would have been to have had it in the archives of the two parishes, there would only have been about half-a-dozen entries in it, starting with that recording the burial of Mrs. Susannah Merrill in 1742. The next had been the secret marriage and various others followed made by Mr. Kinchin. The book, after its appearance at the trial, disappeared into the archives of the solicitors, Elbrow Woodcock, to whom it had been sent at the time.

In 1905, the Rev. Evelyn Heathcote, vicar of Sparsholt and rector of Lainston, determined to see if it could not be found and returned to the parish. He got in touch with Messrs. Bennett and Dawson of 2 New Square, Lincoln's Inn, who, he discovered, had taken over the business of Elbrow Woodcock, only to be told that all the old papers connected with the Woodcocks and their legal affairs had been burned in a fire at the office many years before. It is safe to assume that the Lainston register perished with them.

Elizabeth Chudleigh has suffered a great deal at the hands of her biographers. The present writer has found herself in much the same state as it is said Lytton Strachey found himself when he was writing his biography of Queen Victoria. To begin with, highly critical of her and all she stood for, he found as he went on writing that he was falling in love with her.

Elizabeth Chudleigh was a typical child of an age when 'all the fine ladies' . . . were impulsive and irrational. There was too much excitement, frivolity, love of admiration and notoriety, too much gambling, eating and—too much drinking. Everything was carried to excess and most of all was the offensive affectation of a regard for religion and morality.

INDEX

173